The Spirit Land

Samuel B. Emmons

Alpha Editions

This edition published in 2024

ISBN : 9789361470882

Design and Setting By
Alpha Editions
www.alphaedis.com
Email - info@alphaedis.com

Contents

TO THE READER.

This volume is intended as an antidote to a species of errors that have been rife in every age of the Christian church. Notwithstanding the disclosures the Most High made of himself to his ancient people, they were yet prone to turn aside from the worship of the true God, to follow the lying spirits of the prophets of Baal, and other deceivers, from the days of Moses till the destruction of Jerusalem. So, likewise, under the Christian dispensation, there has been a succession of Antichrists, until their name is *legion*, whose teachings have clouded the understandings and blinded the moral perceptions of men, subverting the faith of many whose mountains stood strong, and who had been counted the chosen people of God.

The present is viewed as an age of *isms*. Men have run mad, and are chasing phantoms. They are roaming round to find some fulcrum to overturn the church and the Bible; they are imagining they are receiving utterances from heaven, when nothing is uttered but the vain fantasies of their own minds and hearts. It is the grossest fanaticism—fanaticism in its most frightful form, leading its unhappy victims, not unfrequently, to flagrant crimes, and to the most horrid of all—that of self-destruction.

These pages are submitted to the public with the counsel of the wisest and best of all ages, that, amid the wily arts of the adversary, we should cling to the word of God, the Bible of our fathers, as the only safe and infallible guide of faith and practice.

NOTE.

We would here give credit to the principal works from which valuable and important matter has been selected for these pages: Whitman's Popular Superstitions; Upham's Lectures upon Witchcraft; Christian Freeman and Family Visitor; Abercrombie on the Intellectual Powers; Influence of the Imagination upon the Nervous System, by Rev. Grant Powers; Life of Adam Clarke; Hayward's Book of all Religions; Miller on the Second Coming of Christ; Borrow's Gypsies of Spain; Stone on False Prophets and Christs; Dickens's Household Words; Capron and Barron on the Spirit Knockings; Dick on the Improvement of Society; Revelations of A. J. Davis; The Great Harmonia; Rogers on Human and Mundane Agents; Miss Crowe's Night Side of Nature; Spiritual Telegraph, &c.

As the work embraces a mass of facts of an absorbing and intensely interesting character, we trust that it will commend itself to an enlightened and judicious public.

THE AUTHOR.

INTRODUCTION.

The object of this treatise upon some of the various errors of the past and present ages is to explain their nature—investigate their origin—describe their injurious effects—and to offer and recommend the necessary measures for their banishment. Most persons, even those who have been well educated, can call to mind the avidity with which, in their days of childhood, they listened to the nursery tales of giants, dwarfs, ghosts, fairies, and witches. The effects of these juvenile impressions are not easily effaced from the mind, and the impressions themselves are but rarely, if ever, forgotten.

To doubt, in former times, the power of charms, and the veracity of omens, and ghost stories, was deemed little less than atheism. The terror caused by them imbittered the lives of persons of all ages. It either served to shut them out of their own houses, or deterred them from going abroad after it was dark. The room in which the head of a family died was for a long time untenanted; particularly if he died without a will, or was supposed to have entertained any peculiar religious opinions. If any disconsolate maiden, or love-crossed bachelor, became the instrument of their own death, the room where the fatal deed was committed was rendered forever uninhabitable, and not unfrequently nailed up. If a drunken farmer, returning from market, fell from his horse, and by the fall broke his own neck, that spot, ever after, was haunted and impassable. In truth, there was scarcely a by-lane or cross-way but had its ghost, which appeared in the shape of a headless cow or horse. Ghosts of a higher degree rode in coaches, drawn by six headless horses, and driven by a headless coachman. As for the churchyards, the legitimate habitations of spectres, clothed all in white, the numbers who swarmed there equalled the living parishioners; and to pass such a place in the night was more perilous than the storming of Badajos.

Confuted and ridiculed as these opinions have been, in later days, the seeds of them are still widely diffused, and at times attempt to spring up in all their earlier excess. In the year 1832, crowds of men, women, and children flocked to the village of Waltham, a few miles from Boston, to see a ghost which was said to make its appearance towards midnight, walking to and fro in a turf meadow, declaring itself, in unearthly tones, to be the spirit of a murdered man, whose bones lay in a mud hole near by. The excitement spread many miles around, and hundreds from the city and neighboring towns hied to the spot, with eyes agape, to behold the solemn visitor from the spirit world. And such was the credulity inspired in the minds of the people, that a clergyman in the vicinity declared from his pulpit, on the following Sabbath, that the awful crime of murder had been revealed by the spirit which had appeared in Waltham! Such is the *excitability* of the mind, and its tendency (notwithstanding the light that has been scattered abroad) to give credence to all the vagaries and nonsense of the darker ages.

CHAPTER I.

THE ORIGIN OF POPULAR SUPERSTITIONS.

Ignorance of correct reasoning has undoubtedly given rise to many superstitions. Inductive reasoning teaches us to infer general conclusions from particular facts which have come under our observation. This definition may be illustrated by an example. You know that water boils on the application of a certain degree of heat. You have seen this experiment tried many times without a single failure. You therefore conclude that water will always boil on the application of this degree of heat, although you have seen it applied but to a small portion of the water in creation. Thus you draw this *general* conclusion from the few *particular* facts which you have witnessed. But had you noticed several failures in the trial, your conclusions would have been doubtful. And if the experiment had failed ninety-nine cases out of a hundred, you would have adopted an opposite conclusion. You would have said that the application of the specified degree of heat would not boil water. In this way, logical reasoning leads to the discovery of truth. Now, apply this principle of sound reasoning to the whole mass of pretended *signs*. Let me select one to show you the absurdity of believing in any. It is commonly reported that the breaking of a looking glass betokens death to some member of the family. This sign probably originated in the following manner: A death happened to follow the breaking of a mirror. Some ignorant person immediately concluded that the breaking of the glass was a sure sign of death. The story soon spread among credulous people, and at length was handed down from generation to generation as an established truth. But you readily perceive the absurdity of forming this *general* conclusion from *one* or a *few* particular facts. We all know that death does not follow the supposed sign oftener than once in a hundred times; and therefore the breaking of the glass is almost a sure sign that no death will immediately take place in the family. But as mirrors are always breaking, and people are always dying, it is not strange that the latter event should sometimes follow the former. It would be a miracle if it did not. But the events have no connection whatever with each other. The coincidence in any case is altogether accidental. We might with the same reason affirm that the breaking of a teakettle is the sign of death, or any thing else, as the breaking of a mirror. But the truth is, there is no sign in the case. It first originated in ignorance of correct reasoning, and has been perpetuated by the credulous. It is but a short time ago that a girl in Exeter, N.H., broke a mirror. She believed that ill luck always followed such an event and therefore became seriously affected in her mind. Finally, her strength failed, and she died a victim to her superstition. Hence we perceive the great importance of a just conception and well-informed judgment upon such apparently trifling, yet oftentimes serious events, in their effects upon social and individual happiness.

We have only to apply this principle of correct reasoning to every sign in existence, to find them to be superstitious. We shall find, upon investigation, that they are based upon no rational evidence, and consequently are not entitled to our belief or confidence. If they indicate any thing, it is something directly opposite to what is generally supposed, for they do not come to pass more than once in a hundred times, and therefore warrant a different conclusion. Not only so. If you believe in the present pretended signs, you may make a million more equally good. A man quarrels after drinking a glass of wine; you may therefore say that taking a glass of wine is the sign of a quarrel. A man draws a prize in a lottery; you may say therefore that the purchase of a ticket is the sign of a fortune. A man dies after supper; you may say therefore that eating supper is the sign of death. In this you may multiply signs to infinity, and they will prove just as true as any now in existence. But our Creator has endowed us with understanding. He has given us reason to regulate our belief by satisfactory evidence. And if we do this, we cannot believe in *any* of the pretended signs. We must conclude that they have all originated in ignorance of correct reasoning, and are kept in remembrance by those who will not use their intellectual powers as their Maker designed.

CHAPTER II.

INDUCTIVE PHILOSOPHY NOT UNDERSTOOD.

Ignorance of inductive philosophy has given rise to many superstitions. By the means of inductive philosophy, we are enabled to trace effects to their true causes. For example: Lights have frequently been seen dancing over marshy grounds, near tan-yards, and burying-places, and along the sea shore. Credulous people have believed them to be the spirits of the uneasy dead. This belief must be considered superstitious, not having any foundation on rational evidence. Philosophy teaches that these lights are occasioned by an inflammable gas, which arises from decayed animal and vegetable substances, and takes fire on coming in contact with atmospheric air. Thus we may trace all effects to their true causes.

Many persons have supposed that pork killed in the increase of the moon would swell in boiling, while that killed in her wane would shrink. This opinion probably originated in the following manner: Some person killed, at different periods of the moon, two hogs which had been born and fattened together. That killed in her increase swelled in boiling; while the other, killed in her wane, shrunk. He could conceive of no way to account for the facts but on the supposition of lunar influence. This conclusion was accordingly adopted, and at length became an established truth. Yet there was no philosophy in forming this opinion from a few such facts. More experiments should have been tried; and they results would have shown that the real cause of the swelling and shrinking existed in the constitution of the animals. It would have been discovered that pork of fine and solid texture would commonly swell, whenever killed; while that of loose and coarse grain would as generally shrink. And the person would no more have thought of attributing the difference in his pork to the moon than to the spirit of Bonaparte.

Let this philosophic principle be applied to this whole class of superstitions, and we shall arrive at similar results. There is the supposed influence of the moon on making soap, grafting trees, cutting timber, and also upon the fortunes of love-sick swains and maidens. The latter are directed to go out in the evening and stand over the bars of a gate, and, looking on the moon, repeat the following lines:—

"All hail to the moon! all hail to thee!

I pray thee, good moon, reveal to me,

This night, who my husband shall be."

They must then go directly to bed, and will dream of their future husband. Upon trial of the experiment, they will probably be inclined to consider it a dreamy notion altogether; for love is of too serious a nature to be fed upon mere *moonshine*.

CHAPTER III.

IGNORANCE OF THE CAUSES OF DREAMS.

Ignorance of the causes of our dreams has given rise to many superstitions. Ancient divines have told us that some of our dreams proceed from ourselves, others from the Deity, and others again from the devil. We know, to be sure, from experience, that dreams proceed from ourselves in *some*, if not in all cases. We admit, however, that God has spoken to some of his dependent creatures by dreams; for we learn this from the Holy Scriptures. But such dreams were direct revelations for the accomplishment of some divine purpose. The volume of revelation was long since closed, and all that is essential to the present and eternal happiness of mankind is plainly revealed. There is therefore no necessity for any further communications from Heaven; and the gospel does not authorize us to expect any. Dreams may sometimes strike a conviction upon the mind, which our waking thoughts may fail to do. And they may sometimes have the appearance of being fulfilled; and yet there may be no necessity of supposing that God has made us the special organ of divine communications. Our dreams, in such cases, may be explained upon the principles of mental philosophy, without resorting to the miraculous interposition of Deity for an explanation.

To say that the devil is the author of all our disagreeable dreams that happen generally when we are in some trouble of body, mind, or estate, is too absurd to believe. And it is specially unbecoming the followers of Jesus to harbor an opinion so unbecoming in itself, so pernicious in its consequences, and so derogatory to the supreme Ruler of the universe. The true doctrine is, that our dreams originate from ourselves. Some are influenced by our bodily sensations. A person with a bottle of hot water at his feet dreams of ascending Ætna; and he finds the heat of the ground almost insupportable. Another kicks the bed clothes from his feet, and dreams of walking through snow banks, even in the summer season. Some dreams are influenced by the state of our stomach and bowels. The hungry prisoner dreams of well-furnished tables and the pleasures of eating. The glutton dreams of a surfeit and its attendant unpleasant sensations. Some dreams are influenced by our dispositions. The person of amiable temper and cheerful spirits is frequently refreshed with delightful scenes and visions of bliss; while those of morose, gloomy, irritable, and melancholy habits are generally harassed with those of a disagreeable and oppressive character. Some dreams are influenced by the state of our health. Sickness is usually productive of those of an unpleasant nature; while health secures those of an opposite description. A gentleman, mentioned by Locke, was not sensible of dreaming till he had a fever, at the age of twenty-six or seven. Some dreams are influenced by our waking thoughts. The mathematician solves difficult problems. The poet roves in Elysian groves. The miser makes great bargains. The sensualist riots in the haunts of dissipation. The criminal sees the dungeon or the gallows. The awakened sinner beholds the flames of hell, or looks upon the sceptre of pardon; and the Christian anticipates heavenly joy.

Strong mental emotions are sometimes embodied into a dream, which, by some natural coincidence, is fulfilled. A murderer, mentioned by Mr. Combe, dreamed of committing murder some years before the event took place. A clergyman on a visit to the city of Edinburgh, from a distance in the country, was sleeping at an inn, when he dreamed of seeing a fire, and one of his children in the midst of it. He awoke with the impression, and instantly started for home. When he arrived within sight of his house, he found it on fire, and got there in time to assist in saving one of his children, who, in the alarm and confusion, had been left in a situation of danger. Without calling in question the possibility of supernatural communications in such cases, this striking occurrence may perhaps be accounted for on simple and natural principles. Let us suppose that the gentleman had a servant who had shown great carelessness in regard to fire, which had often given rise in his mind to a strong apprehension that he might set fire to the house. His anxiety might be increased by being from home, and the same circumstances might make the servant still more careless. Let us further suppose that the gentleman, before going to bed, had, in addition to this anxiety, suddenly recollected that there was on that day, in the neighborhood of his house, some fair or periodical merry making, from which the servant was likely to return home in a state of intoxication. It was most natural that these impressions should be embodied into a dream of his house being on fire, and that the same circumstances might lead to the dream being fulfilled.

The cause of a dream may sometimes be the cause of its fulfilment. A clergyman dreamed of preaching a sermon on a particular subject. In a few weeks, he delivered the discourse. His dream was therefore fulfilled. But his waking thoughts caused the dream, for he had meditated on this very subject; and they also caused its fulfilment, for he proceeded to write and deliver the result of his meditations.

A belief in the supernatural origin of dreams sometimes leads to their fulfilment. A person dreams of approaching sickness. His fears and his imagination hasten on the calamity. A general, on the eve of battle, dreamed of a defeat. His belief in dreams deprived him of courage, and, of course, the enemy conquered. We have on record the case of a German student, who dreamed that he was to die at a certain hour on the next day. His friends found him in the morning making his will and arranging his affairs. As the time drew near, he had every appearance of a person near his end. Every argument was used to shake his belief in the supernatural origin of his dream, but all to no effect. At last, the physician contrived to place the hands of the clock beyond the specified hour, and by this means saved the student's life. There are instances on record where death has actually ensued in consequence of such a belief. It has been produced by the wonderful power the mind possesses over the body. And there can be no doubt that believers in dreams often take the most direct means to hasten their fulfilment.

The apparent fulfilment of dreams is sometimes merely accidental. The dream happens, and the event dreamed of soon follows; but the coincidence is altogether fortuitous. A member of Congress informed a friend that he frequently dreamed of the death of some one of his children, while residing at Washington. The whole scene would appear before him— the sickness, the death, and the burial; and this too several times the same night, and on successive nights. His anxiety for his family caused his dreams. Now, it would have been nothing strange if a member of his family had died. But in this particular instance it was not the case. In this way, however, we are always dreaming of our absent relatives, and it would be singular if a death did not sometimes occur at the time of the dream. So on all other subjects. One event may follow the other, and yet the coincidence be perfectly accidental. There are occasionally some amusing cases of this kind. A person dreamed three times in one night that he must turn to the seventh verse of the fifth chapter of Ecclesiastes, and he would find important instruction. He arose in the morning, and, referring to the specified passage, found these words: "*In the multitude of dreams there are divers vanities.*"

Finally, the occasion of some dreams seems as yet inexplicable. But as we can account for so large a portion of them, it is rational to believe that the causes of the few mysterious ones will be hereafter satisfactorily explained. We think we are safe in believing that all our dreams are caused by some principle of our intellectual or animal nature. Let us then pay no further regard to them than to aim by a pure conscience before God, and a careful attention to our stomachs and health, to have them refreshing and agreeable.

CHAPTER IV.

EFFECTS OF THE IMAGINATION ON THE NERVOUS SYSTEM.

Ignorance of the influence of the imagination upon the nervous system has given rise to many superstitions. We will give a few statements of facts to establish and illustrate this position. Some time previous to 1784, a gentleman in Paris, by the name of Mesmer, professed to have discovered a universal remedy for all diseases; and this remedy consisted in being *magnetized* under peculiar forms and circumstances. M. Mesmer became so noted for his discovery, and he performed such extraordinary cures, that, in 1784, the French king appointed a committee, consisting of four physicians and five members of the Royal Academy of Sciences, to investigate this matter. The committee, as soon as they had examined the whole apparatus employed in magnetizing, and taken cognizance of the manœuvres of Mesmer, and his partner, Deslon, proceeded to notice the symptoms of the patients while under the influence of magnetism. These were various in different individuals. Some were calm and tranquil, and felt nothing; others were affected with coughing and spitting, with pains, heats, and perspirations; and some were agitated and tortured with convulsions. These convulsions were sometimes continued for three hours, accompanied with expectoration of a viscid phlegm, ejected by violent efforts, and sometimes streaked with blood. They had involuntary motions of the limbs, of the whole body, and spasms of the throat. Their eyes wandered in wild motions; they uttered piercing shrieks, wept, laughed, and hiccoughed. The commissioners observed that the great majority of those thus effected were females, and that these exhibitions did not begin until they had been under the operation of magnetism one or two hours, and that, when one became affected, the rest were soon seen in the same situation. In order to give the magnetizer the fairest opportunity to exhibit the power of his invention, and to give the most satisfactory evidence to the public, the commissioners all submitted to be operated upon themselves, and sat under the operation two hours and a half, but without the least effect upon them, except the fatigue of sitting so long in one position. They were magnetized three days in succession, but without any sensible effect being produced. The magnetizing instruments were then removed to Dr. Franklin's house, away from public view, parade, and high expectation, and fourteen persons were then magnetized, all of them invalids. Nine of them experienced nothing, five appeared slightly affected, and the commissioners were surprised to learn, in every instance, that the poor and ignorant alone were affected.

After this eight men and two women were magnetized, but without the least effect. At length a female servant submitted to the same operation, and she affirmed that she felt a heat in every part where the magnetized finger was pointed at her; that she experienced a pain in her head; and, during a continuation of the operation, she became faint, and swooned. When she had fully recovered, they ordered her eyes to be bandaged, and the operator was removed at a distance, when they made her believe that she was still under the operation, and the effects were the same, although no one operated, either near her or at a distance. She could tell the very place where she was magnetized; she felt the same heat in her back and loins, and the same pain in her eyes and ears. At the end of one quarter of an hour, a sign was made for her to be magnetized, but she felt nothing. On the following day, a man and woman were magnetized in a similar manner, and the result was the same. It was found that to direct the *imagination* to the parts where the sensations were to be felt, was all that was necessary to produce these wonderful effects. But *children*, who had not arrived at sufficient maturity of age to be excited by these imposing forms, experienced nothing from the operation.

Mesmer and Deslon asserted that they could magnetize a tree, and every person approaching the tree, in a given time, would be magnetized, and either fall into a swoon or in convulsions, provided the magnetizer was permitted to stand at a distance and direct his look and his cane towards the tree. Accordingly, an apricot tree was selected in Dr. Franklin's garden, at Vassy, for the experiment, and M. Deslon came and magnetized the tree while the patient was retained in the house. The patient was then brought out, with a bandage over his eyes, and successively lead to four trees, which were not magnetized, and was directed to embrace each tree two minutes, while M. Deslon, at a distance, stood pointing his cane to the tree actually magnetized. At the first tree, which was about twenty-seven feet from the magnetized tree, the patient sweat profusely, coughed, expectorated, and said he felt a pain in his head. At the second tree, now thirty feet from the magnetized tree, he found himself giddy, attended with headache, as before. At the third tree, his giddiness and headache were much increased, and he said he believed he was approaching the magnetized tree, although he was still twenty-eight feet from it. At length, when brought to the fourth tree, *not magnetized*, and at the distance of twenty-four feet from that which was, the young man fell down in a state of perfect insensibility; his limbs became rigid, and he was carried to a grass plot, where M. Deslon went to his assistance and recovered him. And yet, in no instance had he approached within a less distance than twenty-four feet of the magnetized tree.

A similar experiment was soon afterwards made on two poor females, at Dr. Franklin's house. These women were separated from each other. Three of the commissioners remained with one of them in one chamber, and two of them with the other, in an adjoining chamber. The first had a bandage over her eyes, and was then made to believe that M. Deslon came in and commenced magnetizing her, although he never entered the room. In three minutes the woman began to shiver. She felt, in succession, a pain in her head, and a pricking in her hands. She became stiff, struck her hands together, got up, stamped, &c., but nothing had been done to her. The woman in the adjoining chamber was requested to take her seat by the door, which was shut, with her sight at liberty. She was then made to believe that M. Deslon would magnetize the door on the opposite side, while the commissioners would wait to witness the result. She had scarcely been seated a minute before she began to shiver. Her breathing became hurried; she stretched out her arms behind her back, writhing them strongly, and bending her body forwards; a general tremor of the whole body came on. The chattering of the teeth was so loud as to be heard out of the room; and she bit her hand so as to leave the marks of her teeth in it; but M. Deslon was not near the door, nor in either chamber, nor was either of the women touched, not even their pulse examined. We perceive, then, that these effects were produced solely by the imagination, and the above facts exhibit very satisfactorily the power which the mind has over the body. The symptoms were not feigned, but, in the peculiar state of mind of these persons, they were involuntary and irresistible. They believed they should be effected in this manner; the idea was formed in their imaginations, and the nerves were acted upon precisely as though what they conceived was real, and the muscular effects followed. And as the patients themselves could not explain the causes of these effects, they very naturally attributed the whole to magnetism. When the commissioners explained the matter, magnetism ceased to produce these wonderful effects. The minds of persons were enlightened upon the subject, and they no longer expected to be influenced in this manner, and accordingly they were not.

Dr. Sigault, an eminent physician of Paris, professed to be an adept in the art of Mesmer. Being at a great assembly one day, he caused it to be announced that he could magnetize. The voice and serious air he assumed had a very sensible effect upon a lady present, although she endeavored at first to conceal the fact. But having carried his hand to the region of the heart, he found it palpitating. She soon experienced difficulty in respiration. The muscles of her face were affected with convulsive twitches; her eyes rolled; she shortly fell down in a fainting fit, vomited her dinner, and experienced incredible weakness and languor. This seemed to corroborate the remarks of Burton, in his *Anatomy of Melancholy*, where he says, "If, by some soothsayer, wise man, fortune teller, or physician, men be told they shall have such a disease, they will so seriously apprehend it that they will instantly labor of it—a thing familiar in China, (saith Riccius, the Jesuit.) If they be told they shall be sick on such a day, when that day comes they will surely be sick, and will be so terribly affected that sometimes they die upon it."

A late English paper states that a young woman, named Winfield, who had been on a visit to Derby, returned home to Radborn, taking a little dog with her by a string. On arriving there, she informed her friends she had seen a gypsy on the road, who told her, that if she led her dog by the string into the house, she would soon be a corpse. Singular to relate, the young woman expired on the following morning! It was thought she died from the effect of imagination, aided by a debilitated constitution.

A missionary among the New Zealanders says, "There is a class of people in New Zealand, called by the natives *Areekee*, and whom we very improperly call *Priests*. These men pretend to have intercourse with departed spirits, by which they are able to kill, by incantation, any person on whom their anger may fall. And it is a fact, that numbers fall a prey to their confidence in the efficacy of the curses of these men, and pine under the influence of despair, and die."

In less than fifteen years after the trial of the pretensions of Mesmer and his coadjutors, in regard to magnetism, there was originated in America, by a Mr. Perkins, a cause of delusion of precisely the same nature. It prevailed in all the United States, in Great Britain, Scotland, and Ireland, and to considerable extent on the continent of Europe. Mr. Perkins prepared two small pieces of different kinds of metal drew them to a point, and polished them. These *Metallic Tractors*, as they were denominated, were said to have, in their joint operation, great power over the electric fluid; and by moving these points gently over the surface of an inflamed part, the heat was extracted, the swelling subsided, and, in a short time, the patient was relieved. After a while, thousands and tens of thousands were ready to certify to the happy influence of these *Tractors*. Mr. Perkins went to England and obtained the royal letters patent, for the purpose of securing to him the advantages of his discovery; and it has been asserted by the best authority, that he returned from England possessed of ten thousand pounds sterling, which he received for the use of his Tractors.

But Dr. Haggarth, an eminent physician and philosopher, recollecting the development of animal magnetism at Paris, wrote to Dr. Falconer, surgeon of the General Hospital at Bath, (England,) and stated his suspicion concerning the Tractors; that their efficacy depended wholly on the imagination of the patient; and recommended the experiment of *wooden* Tractors in the place of the *metallic*.

Accordingly, five persons were selected for the experiment, who were laboring under chronic rheumatism in the ankle, knee, wrist, and hip.

Wooden Tractors were prepared and painted in such a manner that the patients could not discover but that they were metal; and on the 7th of January, 1799, these *wooden* Tractors were employed for the first time. All the patients except one, were relieved. Three were very much benefited. One felt his knee warmer, and he could walk much better, as he showed the medical gentlemen present. One was easier for nine hours, till he went to bed, and then his pain returned. The next day, January 8th, the metallic Tractors were employed with the same effect as that of the preceding day. This led to further experiments of a similar kind, and they were continued, until the physicians became fully satisfied that the wooden Tractors were of the same utility with the metallic, provided the patients *supposed* them metallic. Similar experiments were soon after made at Edinburgh, and the result was the same. A servant girl, afflicted with a most acute headache, which had rendered her nights altogether restless for a fortnight, readily submitted to be pointed at with these *wooden* Tractors. The operator moved them about her head, but did not touch her. In four minutes she felt a chilliness in the head. In a minute or two more, she felt as though cold water was running down her temples, and the pain was diminished. In ten minutes more, she declared that the headache was entirely gone; and the next day she returned to express her thanks to her benefactors for the good sleep she enjoyed through the night. By similar experiments, the intelligent citizens in America soon ascertained the true cause of the deception, and when these facts came to be developed, the Tractors lost all their influence on the human system, and have since been spoken of only in derision.

Here, again, we behold the astonishing power of the imagination over the human system, and witness the miracles that have been performed on the ignorant and unsuspecting. Even in the *modern* practice of the mesmeric art, a great deal of the success depends upon this tendency of the mind. A very respectable operator assures us, that he cannot magnetize persons unless he can first impress them with the belief that they are actually to become magnetized. They must have *faith* in order that the effect may be produced. A public lecturer may hang up his watch before his auditors, and tell them to look upon that watch, and they will become magnetized. Those who expect to be affected are thrown into the magnetic state. Those who have little faith and expectation are seldom, if ever, influenced by such experiments. We, however, do not mean to avow a disbelief in the science of magnetism. On the contrary, we look forward with much interest to its perfection, unencumbered with the false pretensions of its zealous and mistaken friends.

CHAPTER V.

IGNORANCE OF MENTAL PHILOSOPHY.

Ignorance of mental philosophy has given rise to many superstitions. Many persons have believed in the real, visible appearance of ghosts, spirits, or apparitions. Yet these things are clearly and satisfactorily explained on the established principles of mental philosophy. And from this source we learn that they exist alone in the *mind*, in the same manner as do other ideas and images, except in the instances recorded in Scripture. They are caused by some misconception, mental operation, or bodily disorder. We will give a few examples to substantiate this position.

Dr. Ferriar relates the case of a gentleman travelling in the Highlands of Scotland, who was conducted to a bed room which was reported to be haunted by the spirit of a man who had there committed suicide. In the night, he awoke under the influence of a frightful dream, and found himself sitting up in bed with a pistol grasped in his right hand. On looking around the room, he now discovered, by the moonlight, a corpse, dressed in a shroud, reared against the wall, close by the window, the features of the body and every part of the funeral apparel being distinctly perceived. On recovering from the first impulse of terror, so far as to investigate the source of the phantom, it was found to be produced by the moonbeams forming a long, bright image through the broken window.

"Two esteemed friends of mine," says Dr. Abercrombie, "while travelling in the Highlands, had occasion to sleep in separate beds, in one apartment. One of them, having awoke in the night, saw, by the moonlight, a skeleton hanging from the head of his friend's bed, every part of it being perceived in the most distinct manner. He got up to investigate the source of the appearance, and found it to be produced by the moonbeams falling back upon the drapery of the bed, which had been thrown back in some unusual manner, on account of the heat of the weather. He returned to bed, and soon fell asleep. But having awoke again some time after, the skeleton was so distinctly before him, that he could not sleep without again getting up to trace the origin of the phantom. Determined not to be disturbed a third time, he now brought down the curtain to its usual state, and the skeleton appeared no more."

Dr. Dewar relates the case of a lady who was quite blind, and who never walked out without seeing a little old woman, with a crutch and a red cloak, apparently walking before her. She had no illusion when within doors. Dr.

Gregory once took passage in a vessel to a neighboring country, to visit a lady who was in an advanced stage of consumption. On his return, he had taken a moderate dose of laudanum, with the view of preventing seasickness, and was lying on a couch, in the cabin, when the figure of a lady appeared before him in so distinct a manner, that her actual presence could not have been more vivid. He was quite awake, and fully sensible that it was a phantom produced by the opiate, in connection with his intense mental feeling; but he was unable by any effort to banish the vision.

A gentleman, mentioned by Dr. Conolly, when in great danger of being wrecked in a boat, on the Eddystone rocks, said he actually saw his family at the moment. In similar circumstances of great danger, others have described the history of their past lives, being represented to them in such a vivid manner, that, at a single glance, the whole was before them, without the power of banishing the impression. We have read the account of a whole ship's company being thrown into the utmost consternation by the apparition of a cook, who had died a few days before. He was distinctly seen walking ahead of the ship, with a peculiar gait, by which he was distinguished when alive, from having one leg shorter than the other. On steering the ship towards the object, it was found to be a piece of floating wreck!

There is a story on record, of a piratical cruiser having captured a Spanish vessel, during the seventeenth century, and brought her into Marblehead harbor, which was then the site of a few humble dwellings. The male inhabitants were all absent on their fishing voyages. The pirates brought their prisoners ashore, carried them at the dead of night into a solitary glen, and there murdered them. Among the captives was an English female passenger. The women who belonged to the place heard her dying outcries, as they rose through the midnight air, and reverberated far and wide along the silent shores. She was heard to exclaim, "O, mercy, mercy! Lord Jesus Christ, save me! save me!" Her body was buried by the pirates on the spot. The same piercing voice is believed to be heard at intervals, more or less often, almost every year, in the stillness of a calm starlight, or clear moonlight night. There is something, it is said, so wild, mysterious, and evidently superhuman in the sound, as to strike a chill of dread into the hearts of all who listen to it. A writer in the Marblehead Register, of April 3, 1830, declares that "there are not persons wanting at the present day, persons of unimpeachable veracity and known respectability, who still continue to believe the tradition, and to assert that they themselves have been auditors of the sounds described, which they declare were of such an unearthly nature as to preclude the idea of imposition or deception." When "the silver moon holds her way," or when the stars are glistening in the clear, cold sky, and the dark forms of the moored vessels are at rest upon the sleeping bosom of the harbor,—when no natural sound comes forth from the animate or inanimate creation but the dull and melancholy note of the winding shore, how often, at midnight, is the watcher startled from the reveries of an excited imagination by the piteous, dismal, and terrific screams of the unlaid *ghost* of the murdered lady!

Erroneous impressions are often connected with some bodily disease, more especially disease in the brain. Dr. Gregory mentions the case of a gentleman liable to epileptic fits, in whom the paroxysm was generally preceded by the appearance of an old woman in a red cloak, who seemed to come up to him, and strike him on the head with her crutch. At that instant he fell down in the fit. Another is mentioned by Dr. Alderston, of a man who kept a dram shop, and who would often see a soldier endeavoring to force himself into his house in a menacing manner; and in rushing forward to prevent him, would find it a mere phantom. This man was cured by bleeding and purgatives; and the source of this vision was traced to a quarrel which he had had some time before with a drunken soldier. In *delirium tremens* such visions are common, and assume a variety of forms.

Similar phantasms occur in various forms in febrile diseases. A lady was attended by Dr. Abercrombie, having an affection of the chest. She awoke her husband one night, at the commencement of her disorder, and begged him to get up instantly, saying that she had distinctly seen a man enter the apartment, pass the foot of her bed, and go into a closet that entered from the opposite side of the room. She was quite awake, and fully convinced of the reality of the appearance. But, upon examining the closet, it was found to be a delusion, although it was almost impossible to convince the lady it was not a reality.

A writer in the Christian Observer mentions a lady, who, during a severe illness, repeatedly saw her father, who resided at the distance of many hundred miles, come to her bedside, withdraw the curtain, and talk to her in his usual voice and manner. A farmer, mentioned by the same writer, on returning from market, was deeply affected by an extraordinarily brilliant light, which he saw upon the road, and by an appearance in the light, which he supposed to be our Savior. He was greatly alarmed, and, spurring his horse, galloped home; remained agitated during the evening; was seized with typhus fever, then prevailing in the vicinity, and died in about ten days. It was afterwards ascertained, that on the morning of the same day, before he left home, he had complained of headache and languor; and there can be no doubt, says this writer, that the spectral appearance was connected with the commencement of the fever.

Analogous to this is the very striking case related by a physician, of a relative of his, a lady about fifty. On returning home one evening from a party, she went into a dark room to lay aside some part of her dress, when she saw distinctly before her the figure of death, as a skeleton, with his arm uplifted, and a dart in his hand. He instantly aimed a blow at her with the dart, which seemed to strike her on the left side. The same night she was seized with a fever, accompanied with symptoms of inflammation in the left side, but recovered after a severe illness.

We have read the account of a lady who had an illusion affecting both her sight and hearing. She repeatedly heard her husband's voice calling to her by name, as if from an adjoining room. On one occasion, she saw his figure most distinctly, standing before the fire in the drawing room, when he had left the house half an hour before. She went and sat down within two feet of the figure, supposing it to be her husband, and was greatly astonished that he did not answer her when she spoke to him. The figure continued visible several minutes, then moved towards a window at the farther end of the room, and there disappeared. On another occasion, while adjusting her hair before a mirror, late at night, she saw the countenance of a friend, dressed in a shroud, reflected from the mirror, as if looking over her shoulder. This lady had been for some time in bad health, being affected with a lung complaint, and much nervous debility.

Another case of an illusion of hearing is reported of a clergyman, who was accustomed to full living, and was suddenly seized with vomiting, vertigo, and ringing in his ears, and continued in an alarming condition for several days. During this time he heard tunes most distinctly played, and in accurate succession. This patient had, at the same time, a remarkable condition of vision, all objects appearing to him inverted. This peculiarity continued about three days, and ceased gradually; the objects by degrees changing their position, first to the horizontal, and then to the erect.

Some profess to have visions or sights relative to the world of spirits. This was the case with Swedenborg. He relates some of them in the following language: "I dined very late at my lodgings at London, and ate with great appetite, till, at the close of my repast, I perceived a kind of mist about my eyes, and the floor of my chamber was covered with hideous reptiles. They soon disappeared, the darkness was dissipated, and I saw clearly, in the midst of a brilliant light, a man seated in the corner of my chamber, who said to me, in a terrible voice, *Eat not so much.* At these words, my sight became obscured; afterwards it became clear by degrees, and I found myself alone. The night following, the same man, radiant with light, appeared to me, and said, I am God the Lord, Creator and Redeemer. I have chosen you to unfold to men the internal and spiritual sense of the sacred writings, and will dictate to you what you ought to write. At that time, I was not terrified, and the light, although very brilliant, made no unpleasant impression upon my eyes. The Lord was clothed in purple, and the vision lasted a quarter of an hour. The same night, the eyes of my internal man were opened, and fitted to see things in heaven, in the world of spirits, and in hell; in which places I have found many persons of my acquaintance, some of them long since dead, and others lately deceased." In another place, he observes, "I have conversed with apostles, departed popes, emperors, and kings; with the late reformers of the church, Luther, Calvin, and Melancthon, and with others from different countries." In conversing with Melancthon, he wished to know his state in the spirit world, but Melancthon did not see fit to inform him; "wherefore," says Swedenborg, "I was instructed by others concerning his lot, viz., that he is sometimes in an excavated stone chamber, and at other times in hell; and that when in the chamber, he appears to be clothed in a bear's skin by reason of the cold; and that on account of the filth in his chamber, he does not admit strangers from the world, who are desirous of visiting him from the reputation of his name."

The apparitions of Swedenborg were probably caused by his studies, habits, and pursuits. They bear the marks of earthly origin, although he firmly believed they were from heaven. Overloading his stomach at late meals, no doubt, caused some of them. He was in the habit of *eating too much*, as he himself admits. Hence his brain may have been disturbed. We have all heard of the case of an elderly lady, who, being ill, called upon her physician one day for advice. She told him, among other things, that on the preceding night her sleep had been disturbed—that she had seen her grandmother in her dreams. Being interrogated whether she ate any thing the preceding evening, she told the doctor she ate half a mince pie just before going to bed. "Well, madam," said he, "if you had eaten the other half, you might have seen your grandfather also."

The slightest examination of the accounts which remain of occurrences that were deemed supernatural by our ancestors will satisfy any one, at the present day, that they were brought about by causes entirely *natural*, although unknown to them. We will close this part of our investigation by relating the following circumstances, attested by the Rev. James Pierpont, pastor of a church in New Haven:—

"In the year 1647, a new ship of about one hundred and fifty tons, containing a valuable cargo, and several distinguished persons as passengers, put to sea from New Haven in the month of January, bound to England. The vessels that came over the ensuing spring brought no tidings of her arrival in the mother country. The pious colonists were earnest and instant in their prayers that intelligence might be received of the missing vessel. In the course of the following June, a great thunder storm arose out of the north-west; after which, (the hemisphere being serene,) about an hour before sunset, a ship of like dimensions of the aforesaid, with her canvas and colors abroad, (although the wind was northerly,) appeared in the air, coming up from the harbor's mouth, which lies southward from the town, seemingly with her sails filled, under a fresh gale, holding her course north, and continuing under observation, sailing against the wind, for the space of half an hour. The phantom ship was borne along, until, to the excited imaginations of the spectators, she seemed to have approached so near that they could throw a stone into her. Her main topmast then disappeared, then her mizzen topmast, then her masts were entirely carried away, and finally her hull fell off, and vanished from sight, leaving a dull and smoke-colored cloud, which soon dissolved, and the whole atmosphere became clear. All affirmed that the airy vision was a precise copy of the missing vessel, and that it was sent to announce and describe her fate. They considered it the spectre of the lost ship, and the Rev. Mr. Davenport declared in public 'that God had condescended, for the quieting of their afflicted spirits, this extraordinary account of his sovereign disposal of those for whom so many fervent prayers were made continually.'"

The results of modern science enable us to explain the mysterious appearance. It is probable that some Dutch vessel, proceeding slowly, quietly, and unconsciously on her voyage from Amsterdam to the New Netherlands, happened at the time to be passing through the Sound. At the moment the apparition was seen in the sky, she was so near, that her image was painted or delineated to the eyes of the observers, on the clouds, by the laws of optics, now generally well known, before her actual outlines could be discerned by them on the horizon. As the sun sunk behind the western hills, and his rays were gradually withdrawn, the visionary ship slowly disappeared, and the approach of the night, while it dispelled the vapors from the atmosphere, effectually concealed the vessel as she continued her course along the Sound.

The optical illusions that present themselves, on the sea shore, by which distant objects are raised to view, the opposite islands and capes made to loom up, lifted above the line of the apparent circumference of the earth, and thrown into every variety of shape which the imagination can conceive, are among the most beautiful phenomena of nature, and they impress the mind with the idea of enchantment and mystery, more perhaps than any others. But they have received a complete solution from modern discovery.

It should be observed that the optical principles that explain these phenomena have recently afforded a foundation for the science, or rather the *art*, of *nauscopy*. There are persons, it is said, in some places in the Isle of France, whose calling and profession it is to ascertain and predict the approach of vessels by their reflection in the atmosphere and on the clouds, long before they are visible to the eye or through the glass.

Our vision is at all times liable to be disturbed by atmospheric conditions. So long as the atmosphere between our person and the object we are looking at is of the same density, we may be said to see in a straight line to the object. But if, by any cause, a portion of that atmosphere is rendered less or more dense, the line of vision is bent, or refracted, from its course. A thorough comprehension of this truth in science has banished a mass of superstition. It has been found that, by means of powerful refraction, objects at great distances, and round the back of a hill, or considerably beneath the horizon, are brought into sight. In some countries this phenomenon is called *mirage*. The following is one of the most interesting and best-authenticated cases of the kind. In a voyage performed by Captain Scoresby, in 1822, he was able to recognize his father's ship, when below the horizon, from the inverted image of it which appeared in the air. "It was," says he, "so well defined, that I could distinguish, by a telescope, every sail, the general rig of the ship, and its particular character, insomuch that I confidently pronounced it to be my father's ship, the Fame,—which it afterwards proved to be—though on comparing notes with my father, I found that our relative position, at the time, gave our distance from one another very nearly thirty miles, being about seventeen miles beyond the horizon, and some leagues beyond the limit of direct vision!"

Dr. Vince, an English philosopher, was once looking through a telescope at a ship which was so far off that he could only see the upper part of the masts. The hull was entirely hidden by the bending of the water; but, between himself and the ship, he saw two perfect images of it in the air. These were of the same form and color as the real ship; but one of them was turned completely upside down.

In the sandy plains of Egypt, the mirage is seen to great advantage. These plains are often interrupted by small eminences, upon which the inhabitants have built their villages in order to escape the inundations of the Nile. In the morning and evening, objects are seen in their natural form and position; but when the surface of the sandy ground is heated by the sun, the land seems terminated, at a particular distance, by a general inundation; the villages which are beyond it appear like so many islands in a great lake; and an inverted image of a village appears between the hills.

The Swedish sailors long searched for a supposed magic island, which, from time to time, could be descried between the Island of Aland and the coast of Upland. It proved to be a rock, the image of which was presented in the air by mirage. At one time, the English saw, with terror, the coast of Calais and Boulogne, in France, rising up on the opposite side of the Channel, and apparently approaching their island. But the most celebrated example of mirage is exhibited in the Straits of Messina. The inhabitants of the Calabrian shore behold images of palaces, embattled ramparts, houses, and ships, and all the varied objects of towns and landscapes, in the air— being refracted images from the Sicilian coast. This wonderful phenomenon is superstitiously regarded by the common people as the work of fairies.

CHAPTER VI.

IGNORANCE OF TRUE RELIGION.

Ignorance of true religion has given rise to many prevailing superstitions. The Savior has taught us that the Father of spirits regulates the minutest events of this world, and that he alone is the Supreme Ruler of the universe. Our experience and observation must convince us that this infinite work is accomplished by regular laws, and that Infinite Wisdom sees fit so to govern all events without the intervention of miracles, or through the agency of any instrumentality but his own. And by examination, we shall find that these truths are in direct opposition to the general mass of popular superstitions.

There are many who believe in signs. They believe that the howling of a dog under a window betokens death to some member of the family. But how does the dog obtain this foreknowledge? Who sends him on this solemn errand? If you say that his appearance at the house is accidental, then you would have us trust to *chance* for information upon this most important subject. If you say that his knowledge of the approaching event is intuitive, then you would have us believe that the irrational brute knows more than his intelligent master. If you say that he is instigated by some wicked spirit, then you would have us admit that an enemy of mankind is more attentive to their welfare than God; for it certainly betokens the greatest kindness to notify us of our near dissolution. If you say the animal is sent by God, how will you explain the fact that the sign so often fails? not actually taking place oftener, at most, than once in a hundred times. Certainly we are not to accuse the omniscient and merciful Jehovah either of ignorance concerning future events, or of trifling with the feelings of his dependent creatures. We must therefore consider the sign to be altogether superstitious, and contrary to all rational evidence.

Some persons profess to believe in lucky and unlucky days. They say, for instance, that Friday is an unlucky day. And why so? Does God part with the reins of his government, and employ wicked spirits to torment his creatures on this day? Does he make this day more unpropitious to human affairs than others? Do facts go to show that more disasters occur on this day than on any other? Paul instructs us that all days are alike, and that God rules the universe with infinite wisdom and benevolence. Then why should we account Friday to be an unlucky day? Whence came such an opinion? From heathenism. The heathen were much influenced by this superstition; and when converted to Christianity, they incorporated this among some other absurdities into their religious belief. Because our Savior was crucified on Friday, they placed this at the head of their unlucky days. But why they did so, we cannot conceive; for the death of Christ was absolutely necessary for the deliverance of mankind from sin and death. And for this reason alone, Friday was the most propitious day that ever dawned upon a dying world. But the heathen converts did not consider this circumstance. They pronounced Sunday, the day of his resurrection, to be the most fortunate. Later Christians, in a certain sense, have thought differently. Sir Matthew Hale has remarked, that he never knew any undertaking to prosper that was commenced on the Sabbath. And the early laws of Connecticut prohibited any vessel from either leaving a port, or entering a port, or passing by a village on Sunday. But such prohibitions are not agreeable to the notions of seamen, who, as a class, are inclined to be somewhat superstitious. We frequently meet with dissipated, unbelieving sailors, who could not be induced to put to sea on Friday on any consideration; but who would rather labor seven successive nights than not sail on the Sabbath. It is rather singular that sceptics should be so afraid of the day of our Savior's crucifixion, and so fond of that of his resurrection. Such inconsistency, however, is not uncommon. Those who rail most at the credulity of others are frequently the most superstitious. Those who lay the greatest claims to bravery are, for the most part, the greatest cowards. Voltaire could ridicule religion in fair weather, but the moment a thunder cloud appeared, he was thrown into extreme consternation, and must have a priest to pray during its continuance for his preservation. If we would avoid the influence of this heathen superstition, we must regard *actions* rather than *days*. If our engagements are *proper*, we have nothing to fear from the day on which they are commenced. If we feel the evidence within that God is indeed *our* Father, we shall not be prevented, by any belief in lucky or unlucky days, from doing our duty on every day, and enjoying peace and happiness on all days.

CHAPTER VII.

BELIEF IN WITCHCRAFT.

A witch was regarded by our fathers as a person who had made an actual, deliberate, and formal contract with Satan, by which contract it was agreed that the party should become his faithful subject, and do whatever should be required in promoting his cause. And in consideration of this allegiance and service, he, on his part, agreed to exercise his supernatural powers in the person's behalf. It was considered as a transfer of allegiance from God to the devil. The agreement being concluded, Satan bestows some trifling sum of money to bind the bargain; then, cutting or pricking a finger causes the individual to sign his or her name, or make the mark of a cross, with their own blood, on a piece of parchment. In addition to this signature, in some places, the devil made the witches put one hand to the crown of their head, and the other to the sole of the foot, signifying they were entirely his. Before the devil quits his new subject, he delivers to her or him an imp or familiar, and sometimes two or three. They are of different shapes and forms, some resembling a cat, others a mole, a miller fly, spider, or some other insect or animal. These are to come at bidding, to do such mischief as the witch may command, and, at stated times of the day, suck the blood of the witch, through teats, on different parts of the body. Feeding, suckling, or rewarding these imps was, by law, declared *felony*.

Sometimes a witch, in company with others of the fraternity, is carried through the air on brooms or spits, to distant meetings or Sabbaths of witches. But for this they must anoint themselves with a certain magical ointment given them by the devil. Lord Bacon, in his philosophical works, gives a recipe for the manufacture of an ointment that enabled witches to fly in the air. It was composed of the fat of children, digged out of their graves, and of the juices of smaltage, cinquefoil, and wolfsbane, mixed with meal of fine wheat. After greasing themselves with this preparation, the witches flew up chimney, and repaired to the spot in some graveyard or dismal forest, where they were to hold their meetings with the evil one. At these meetings they have feasting and dancing, the devil himself sometimes condescending to play on the great fiddle, pipe, or harp. When the meeting breaks up, they all have the honor of kissing his majesty, who for that ceremony usually assumes the form of a he goat.

Witches showed their spite by causing the object of it to waste away in a long and painful disease, with a sensation of thorns stuck in the flesh. Sometimes they caused their victims to swallow pins, old nails, dirt, and trash of all sorts, invisibly conveyed to them by their imps. Frequently they showed their hate by drying up the milk of cows, or by killing oxen. For slight offences they would prevent butter from coming in the churn, or beer from working. Grace Greenwood says, that, on a visit to Salem in the fall of 1850, she "was shown a vial of the veritable bewitched pins with which divers persons were sorely pricked by the wicked spite of certain witches and wizards."

It was believed that Satan affixed his mark or seal to the bodies of those in allegiance with him, and that the spot where this mark was made became callous and dead. In examining a witch upon trial, they would pierce the body with pins, and if any spot was found insensible to the torture, it was looked upon as ocular demonstration of guilt. Another method to detect a witch, was to weigh her against the church Bible. If she was guilty, the Bible would preponderate. Another was by making her say the Lord's prayer, which no one actually possessed could do correctly. A witch could not weep but three tears, and that only out of the left eye; and this was considered by many an decisive proof of guilt. But swimming was the most infallible ordeal. They were stripped naked, and bound the right thumb to the left toe, and the left thumb to the right toe. Being thus prepared, they were thrown into a pond or river. If guilty, they could not sink; for having, by their compact with the devil, renounced the water of baptism, that element renounces them, and refuses to receive them into its bosom.

In 1664, a man by the name of Matthew Hopkins, in England, was permitted to explore the counties of Essex, Suffolk, and Huntingdon, with a commission to discover witches, receiving twenty shillings from each town he visited. Many persons were pitched upon, and through his means convicted. At length, some gentlemen, out of indignation at his barbarity, tied him in the same manner he had bound others, thumbs and toes together, in which state, putting him in the water, he swam! Standing condemned on his own principles, the country was rescued from the power of his malicious imposition.

The subsequent illustration of the condition of religion less than two hundred years ago will excite a few humbling thoughts. In the parish register of Glammis, Scotland, June, 1676, is recorded—"Nae preaching here this Lord's day, the minister being at Gortachy, burning a witch." Forty thousand persons, it is said, were put to death for witchcraft in England during the seventeenth century, and a much greater number in Scotland, in proportion to its population.

In 1692, the whole population of Salem and vicinity were under the influence of a terrible delusion concerning witchcraft. By yielding to the sway of their credulous fancies, allowing their passions to be worked up to a tremendous pitch of excitement, and running into excesses of folly and violence, they have left a dark stain upon their memory, that will awaken a sense of shame, pity, and amazement in the minds of their latest posterity. The principal causes that led to their delusion, and to the proceedings connected with it, were, a proneness to superstition, owing in a great degree to an ignorance of natural science, too great a dependence upon the imagination, and the power of sympathy. In contemplating the errors and sufferings which ignorance of philosophy and science brought upon our fathers, we should be led to appreciate more gratefully, and to improve with more faithfulness, our own opportunities to acquire wisdom and knowledge. But we would not be understood as saying, that mere intellectual cultivation is sufficient to banish every superstition. No. For who were ever better educated than the ancient Greeks and Romans? And yet, who were ever more influenced by a belief in signs, omens, spectres, and witches? We believe that, when the gospel, in its purity and simplicity, shall shed its divine light abroad, and pervade the hearts of men, superstition, in all its dark and hideous forms, will recede, and vanish from the world.

In concluding our remarks under this head, we would add that, in a dictionary before us, a witch is designated as a woman, and *wizard* as a man, that pretends to some power whereby he or she can foretell future events, cure diseases, call up or drive away spirits. The art itself is called *witchcraft*. If this is a correct definition, witches and wizards are quite a numerous class of people in society at the present day; for there are many among us who presume to practise these things.

CHAPTER VIII.

NECROMANCY AND FORTUNE TELLING.

Although the belief in witchcraft has nearly passed away, the civilized world is yet full of necromancers and fortune tellers. The mystic science of "palmistry" is still practised by many a haggard and muttering vagrant.

The most celebrated fortune teller, perhaps, that ever lived, resided in Lynn, Mass. The character of "Moll Pitcher" is familiarly known in all parts of the commercial world. She died in 1813. Her place of abode was beneath the projecting and elevated summit of High Rock, in Lynn, and commanded a view of the wild and indented coast of Marblehead, of the extended and resounding beaches of Lynn and Chelsea, of Nahant Rocks, of the vessels and islands, of Boston's beautiful bay, and of its remote southern shore. She derived her mysterious gifts by inheritance, her grandfather having practised them before, in Marblehead. Sailors, merchants, and adventurers of every kind visited her residence, and placed great confidence in her predictions. People came from great distances to learn the fate of missing friends or recover the possession of lost goods. The young, of both sexes, impatient at the tardy pace of time, and burning with curiosity to discern their future lot, especially as it regarded matters of wedlock, availed themselves of every opportunity to visit her lowly dwelling, and hear from her prophetic lips the revelations of these most tender incidents and important events of their coming lives. She read the future, and traced what, to mere mortal eyes, were the mysteries of the present or the past, in the arrangement and aspect of the grounds or settlings of a cup of tea or coffee. Her name has every where become the generic title of fortune tellers, and occupies a conspicuous place in the legends and ballads of popular superstition.

A man was suddenly missed by his friends from a certain town in this commonwealth. The church immediately sent a member to consult the far-famed fortune-telling Molly Pitcher. After making the necessary inquiries, she intimated that the absent person had been murdered by a family of negroes, and his body sunk in the deep waters behind their dwelling. Upon this evidence, the accused were forthwith imprisoned, and the pond raked in vain, from shore to shore. A few days previous to the trial, the missing man returned to his friends, safe and sound; thus proving that the fortune teller, instead of having received from Satan certain information of distant and unknown events, actually played off a piece of the grossest deception upon her credulous visitors.

We are told by travellers that there is scarcely a village in Syria in which there is not some one who has the credit of being able to cast out evil spirits. About eight miles from the ancient Sidon, Lady Hester Stanhope, the granddaughter of the immortal Chatham, and niece of the equally immortal Pitt, recently lived in a style of Eastern splendor and magnificence. She spent her time in gazing at the extended canopy of heaven, as it shed its sparkling light upon the ancient hills and sacred groves of Palestine—her soul absorbed in the fathomless mysteries of her loved astrology, and holding fancied communion with supernatural powers and spirits of the departed.

There recently died in Hopkinton, Mass., an individual by the name of Sheffield, who had long followed the art of fortune telling by astrology. He professed to unfold almost every secret, or mystery, even to foretelling the precise day and hour any person would die. In case of lost or stolen goods, it was only necessary to enclose a small fee in a letter, containing also a statement of your name, age, and place of residence, and forward the same by mail to his address. In two or three weeks, the information you sought, as to the person who stole the property, &c., would be forwarded to you, leaving you to judge of the case for yourself. He did quite a business in his line, and made something of a fortune out of a long-exploded science.

There are many who trust to the declarations of such persons, and are often made unhappy thereby. In fact, it is doubtful if a more unhappy class can be found than those who are in the habit of consulting fortune tellers of any character. It is *discontent*, chiefly, that leads them to pry into futurity. And after having had their *fortunes told*, as it is termed, they are no better satisfied than before; for the best of fortune tellers are famous for their errors and mistakes, although it would be strange if they did not blunder upon some facts in the whole routine of their business. But we pity those who rely upon their prognostications. If told they will die at such or such a time, or if they are to meet with some dreadful accident, misfortune, or disappointment, their imaginations will lead them to anticipate and dread the event, which will be the surest way to produce its fulfilment. If a husband or wife is told that he or she will marry again, it will lead them to be dissatisfied with the partner with whom they are at present associated. And look at this subject as we will, we shall find it productive of a vast amount of evil, and therefore deserving of our entire disapprobation.

CHAPTER IX.

FAIRIES, OR WANDERING SPIRITS.

Fairies, says a certain author, are a sort of intermediate beings, between men and women, having bodies, yet with the power of rendering them *invisible*, and of passing through all sorts of enclosures. They are remarkably small of stature, with fair complexions, whence they derive their name, *fairies*. Both male and female are generally clothed in green, and frequent mountains, the sunny side of hills, groves, and green meadows, where they amuse themselves with dancing, hand in hand, in a circle, by moonlight. The traces of their feet are said to be visible, next morning, on the grass, and are commonly called *fairy rings*, or *circles*.

Fairies have all the passions and wants of men, and are great lovers of cleanliness and propriety; for the observance of which, they frequently reward servants, by dropping money in their shoes. They likewise punish sluts and slovens by pinching them black and blue. They often change their weak and starveling elves, or children, for the more robust offspring of men. But this can only be done before baptism; for which reason it is still the custom, in the Highlands, to watch by the cradle of infants till they are christened. The word *changeling*, now applied to one almost an idiot, attests the current belief of these superstitious mutations.

Some fairies dwell in mines, and in Wales nothing is more common than these subterranean spirits, called *knockers*, who very good naturedly point out where there is a rich vein of lead or silver. In Scotland there was a sort of domestic fairies, from their sun-burnt complexions, called *brownies*. These were extremely useful, performing all sorts of domestic drudgery.

In the Life of Dr. Adam Clarke, we have the following account of a circumstance that took place in the town of Freshford, county of Kilkenny, Ireland, showing the superstition prevailing in that country concerning the influence of these fairy beings: "A farmer built himself a house of three apartments, the kitchen in the middle, and a room for sleeping, &c., on either end. Some time after it was finished, a cow of his died—then a horse; to these succeeded other smaller animals, and last of all his *wife* died. Full of alarm and distress, supposing himself to be an object of *fairy indignation*, he went to the *fairy man*, that is, one who pretends to know *fairy* customs, haunts, pathways, antipathies, caprices, benevolences, &c., and he asked his advice and counsel on the subject of his losses. The wise man, after having considered all things, and cast his eye upon the house, said, 'The fairies, in their night walks from *Knockshegowny* Hill, in county *Tipperary*, to the county of *Kilkenny*, were accustomed to pass over the very spot where one of your rooms is now built; you have blocked up their way, and they were very angry with you, and have slain your cattle, and killed your wife, and, if not appeased, may yet do worse harm to you.' The poor fellow, sadly alarmed, went, and with his own hands, deliberately pulled down the timbers, demolished the walls, and left not one stone upon another, but razed the very foundation, and left the path of these capricious gentry as open and as clear as it was before. How strong must have been this man's belief in the existence of these demi-natural and semi-supernatural beings, to have induced him thus to destroy the work of his own hands!"

In Spenser's epic poem, called the Fairy Queen, the imagination of the reader is entertained with the characters of fairies, witches, magicians, demons, and departed spirits. A kind of pleasing horror is raised in the mind, and one is amused with the strangeness and novelty of the persons who are represented in it; but to be affected by such poetry requires an odd turn of thought, a peculiar cast of fancy, with an imagination naturally fruitful and superstitious.

The Gypsies are a class of strolling beggars, cheats, and fortune tellers. They have been quite numerous in all the older countries, and are so still in some of them; but in the United States there are but few, some one or two tribes in the west, and a small party of them in New York state. They are probably called Gypsies from the ancient Egyptians, who had the character of great cheats, whence the name might afterwards pass proverbially into other languages, as it did into the Greek and Latin; or else the ancient Egyptians being much versed in astronomy, or rather astrology, the name was afterwards assumed by these modern fortune tellers. In Latin they are called *Egyptii*; the Italians called them *Cinari*, or *Cingani*; the Russians, *Zigani*; the Turks and Persians, *Zingarri*; the Germans, *Ziguenor*; the Spaniards, *Gitános*; the French, *Bohemians*, from the circumstance that Bohemia was the first civilized country where they made their appearance.

In most countries they live in the woods and forests; but in England, where every inch of land is cultivated, the covered cart and little tent are their houses, and they seldom remain more than three days in the same place.

Dabbling in sorcery is in some degree the province of the female Gypsy. She affects to tell the future, and to prepare philters, by means of which love can be awakened in any individual towards any particular object; and such is the credulity of the human race, even in the most enlightened countries, that the profits arising from these practices are great. The following is a case in point: Two females, neighbors and friends, were tried, some years since, for the murder of their husbands. It appeared that they were in love for the same individual, and had conjointly, at various times, paid sums of money to a Gypsy woman to work charms to captivate his affections. Whatever little effect the charms might produce, they were successful in their principal object, for the person in question carried on for some time a criminal intercourse with both. The matter came to the knowledge of the husbands, who, taking means to break off this connection, were both poisoned by their wives. Till the moment of conviction, these wretched females betrayed neither emotion nor fear; but at this juncture their consternation was indescribable. They afterwards confessed that the Gypsy, who had visited them in prison, had promised to shield them from conviction by means of her art. It is therefore not surprising that in the fifteenth and sixteenth centuries, when a belief in sorcery was supported by the laws of all Europe, these people were regarded as practisers of sorcery, and punished as such, when, even in the nineteenth, they still find people weak enough to place confidence in their claims to supernatural power.

In telling fortunes, the first demand of the Gypsy, in England, is invariably a sixpence, in order that she may cross her hands with silver; and here the same promises are made, and as easily believed, as in other countries, leading to the conclusion that mental illumination, amongst the generality of mankind, has made no progress whatever; as we observe in the nineteenth century the same gross credulity manifested as in the seventeenth, and the inhabitants of one of the countries most celebrated for the arts of civilization imposed upon by the same stale tricks which served to deceive, two centuries before, in Spain, a country whose name has long and justly been considered as synonymous with every species of ignorance and barbarity.

In telling fortunes, promises are the only capital requisite, and the whole art consists in properly adapting these promises to the age and condition of the parties who seek for information. The Gitános are clever enough in the accomplishment of this, and generally give perfect satisfaction. Their practice lies chiefly amongst females, the portion of the human race most given to curiosity and credulity. To the young maidens they promise lovers, handsome invariably, and oftentimes rich; to wives, children, and perhaps another husband; for their eyes are so penetrating, that occasionally they will develop your most secret thoughts and wishes; to the old, riches, and nothing but riches—for they have sufficient knowledge of the human heart to be aware that avarice is the last passion that becomes extinct within it. These riches are to proceed either from the discovery of hidden treasure, or from across the water. The Gitános, in the exercise of this practice, find dupes almost as readily amongst the superior classes, as the veriest dregs of the population.

They are also expert in chiromancy, which is the determining, from certain lines upon the hand, the quality of the physical and intellectual powers of the possessor, to which lines they give particular and appropriate names, the principal of which is called the "line of life." An ancient writer, in speaking of this art, says, "Such chiromancy is not only reprobated by theologians, but by men of law and physic, as a foolish, vain, scandalous, futile, superstitious practice, smelling much of divinery and a pact with the devil."

The Gitános in the olden time appear to have not unfrequently been subjected to punishment as sorceresses, and with great justice, as the abominable trade which they have always driven in philters and decoctions certainly entitled them to that appellation, and to the pains and penalties reserved for those who practised what is generally termed "witchcraft."

Amongst the crimes laid to their charge, connected with the exercise of occult powers, there is one of a purely imaginary character, which if they were ever punished for, they had assuredly but little right to complain, as the chastisement they met with was fully merited by practices equally malefic as the one imputed to them, provided that were possible. *It was the casting the evil eye.*

In the Gitáno language, casting the evil eye is called *querelar nasula*, which simply means making sick, and which, according to the common superstition, is accomplished by casting an evil look at people, especially children, who, from the tenderness of their constitution, are supposed to be more easily blighted than those of a more mature age. After receiving the evil glance, they fall sick, and die in a few hours.

In Andalusia, a belief in the evil eye is very prevalent among the lower orders. A stag's horn is considered a good safeguard, and on that account, a small horn, tipped with silver, is frequently attached to the children's necks, by means of a cord braided from the hair of a black mare's tail. Should the evil glance be cast, it is imagined that the horn receives it, and instantly snaps asunder. Such horns may be purchased at the silversmiths' shops at Seville.

The Gypsies sell remedies for the evil eye, which consist of any drugs which they happen to possess, or are acquainted with. They have been known to offer to cure the glanders in a horse, (an incurable disorder,) with the very same powders which they offer as a specific for the evil eye.

The same superstition is current among all Oriental people, whether Turks, Arabs, or Hindoos; but perhaps there is no nation in the world with whom the belief is so firmly rooted as the Jews; it being a subject treated of in all the old rabbinical writings, which induces the conclusion that the superstition of the evil eye is of an antiquity almost as remote as the origin of the Hebrew race.

The evil eye is mentioned in Scripture, but not in the false and superstitious sense we have spoken of. Evil in the eye, which occurs in Prov. xxiii. 5, 6, merely denotes niggardness and illiberality. The Hebrew words are *ain ra*, and stand in contradistinction to *ain toub*, or the benignant in eye, which denotes an inclination to bounty and liberality.

The rabbins have said, "For one person who dies of sickness, there are ten who die by the evil eye." And as the Jews, especially those of the East, and of Barbary, place implicit confidence in all that the rabbins have written, we can scarcely wonder if, at the present day, they dread this visitation more than the cholera or the plague. "The leech," they say, "can cure those disorders; but who is capable of curing the evil eye?"

It is imagined that this blight is most easily inflicted when a person is enjoying himself, with little or no care for the future, when he is reclining in the sun before his door, or when he is full of health and spirits, but principally when he is eating and drinking, on which account the Jews and Moors are jealous of strangers when they are taking their meals.

"I was acquainted," says a late writer, "with a very handsome Jewess, of Fez; she had but one eye, but that one was particularly brilliant. On asking her how she lost its fellow, she informed me that she was once standing in the street, at nightfall, when she was a little girl; a Moor, that was passing by, suddenly stopped, and said, 'Towac Ullah, (blessed be God,) how beautiful are your eyes, my child!' Whereupon she went into the house, but was presently seized with a dreadful pain in the left eye, which continued during the night, and the next day the pupil came out of the socket. She added, that she did not believe the Moor had any intention of hurting her, as he gazed on her so kindly; but that it was very thoughtless in him to utter words which are sure to convey evil luck." It is said to be particularly dangerous to eat in the presence of a woman; for the evil eye, if cast by a woman, is far more fatal and difficult to cure than if cast by a man.

When any one falls sick of the evil eye, he must instantly call to his assistance the man cunning in such cases. The man, on coming, takes either a girdle or a handkerchief from off his own person, and ties a knot at either end; then he measures three spans with his left hand, and at the end of these three he fastens a knot, and folds it three times round his head, pronouncing this *beraka*, or blessing: "*Ben porat Josef, ben porat ali ain*," (Joseph is a fruitful bough, a fruitful bough by a well;) he then recommences measuring the girdle or handkerchief, and if he finds three spans and a half, instead of the three which he formerly measured, he is enabled to tell the name of the person who cast the evil eye, whether male or female.

The above very much resembles the charm of the Bible and key, by which many persons in England still pretend to be able to discover the thief, when an article is missed. A key is placed in a Bible, in the part called Solomon's Song; the Bible and key are then fastened strongly together, by means of a ribbon, which is wound round the Bible, and passed several times through the handle of the key, which projects from the top of the book. The diviner then causes the person robbed to name the name of any person or persons whom he may suspect. The two parties, the robbed and the diviner, then standing up, support the book between them, the ends of the handle of the key resting on the tips of the fore fingers of the right hand. The diviner then inquires of the Bible, whether such a one committed the theft, and commences repeating the sixth and seventh verses of the eighth chapter of the Song; and if the Bible and key turn round in the mean time, the person named is considered guilty. This charm has been, and still is, the source of infinite mischief, innocent individuals having irretrievably lost their character among their neighbors from recourse being had to the Bible and key. The slightest motion of the finger, or rather of the nail, will cause the key to revolve, so that the people named are quite at the mercy of the diviner, who is generally a cheat, or professed conjurer, and not unfrequently a Gypsy. In like manner, the Barbary cunning man, by a slight contraction of his hand, measures three and a half spans, where he first measured three, and then pretends to know the person who has cast the evil eye, having, of course, first ascertained the names of those with whom his patient has lately been in company.

When the person who has cast the evil eye has been discovered, by means of the magical process already described, the mother, or wife, or sister of the sufferer walks forth, pronouncing the name of the latter with a loud voice, and, making the best of her way to the house of the person guilty, takes a little of the earth from before the door of his or her sleeping apartment. Some of the saliva of the culprit is then demanded, which must be given early in the morning, before breakfast; then the mother, or the wife, or the sister goes to the oven, and takes from thence seven burning coals, which are slaked in water from the bath in which the women bathe. The four ingredients, earth, saliva, coals, and water, are then mixed together in a dish, and the patient is made to take three sips, and what remains is taken to a private place and buried, the person who buries it making three paces backward, exclaiming, "May the evil eye be buried beneath the earth." Many people carry papers about with them, scrawled with hieroglyphics, which are prepared by the hacumim, or sages, and sold. These papers, placed in a little bag and hung about the person, are deemed infallible preservatives from the "ain ara."

Like many other superstitions, the above may be founded on a physical reality. In hot countries, where the sun and moon are particularly dazzling, the belief in the evil eye is most prevalent. If we turn to the Scripture, we shall probably come to the solution of the belief. "The sun shall not smite thee by day, nor the moon by night." Ps. cxxi. 5, 6. To those who loiter in the sunshine, before the king of day has nearly reached his bourn in the west, the sun has an evil eye, and his glance produces brain fevers; and to those who sleep uncovered, beneath the smile of the moon, her glance is poisonous, producing insupportable itching in the eye and not unfrequently total blindness: all the charms, scrawls, and rabbinical antidotes have no power to avert these effects.

The northern nations have a superstition which bears some resemblance to the evil eye. They have no brilliant sun and moon to addle the brain and poison the eye, but the gray north has its marshes, and fenny ground, and fetid mists, which produce agues, low fevers, and moping madness, and are as fatal to cattle as to man. Such disorders are attributed to elves and fairies. This superstition still lingers in some parts of England, under the name of *elf-shot*, whilst, throughout the north, it is called *elle-skiod*, and *elle-vild*, (fairy wild.) It is particularly prevalent amongst shepherds and cowherds, who, from their manner of life, are most exposed to the effects of the so called elf-shot.

The Gitános had a venomous preparation called *drao*, or *drow*, which they were in the habit of flinging into the mangers of the cattle, for the purpose of causing sickness and death. It was the province of the women to compound the ingredients of this poison, which answered many wicked purposes. The stalls and stables were visited secretly, and the provender of the animals being poisoned, they at once fell sick; speedily there appeared the Gitános, offering their services on the condition of no cure no pay, and when these were accepted, the malady was speedily removed. They used no medicines, or pretended not to, but charms only, which consisted of small variegated beans, called, in their language, *bobis*, coming from a Russian word signifying *beans*. These beans they dropped into the mangers, though they doubtless administered privately a real and efficacious remedy. By these means they fostered the idea, already prevalent, that they were people possessed of supernatural gifts and powers. By means of drao, they likewise procured themselves food; poisoning swine, as their brethren in England still do, and then feasting on the flesh, the poison only affecting the head of the animal, which was abandoned as worthless; witness one of their own songs:—

"By Gypsy drow the porker died;

I saw him stiff at evening tide;

But I saw him not when morning shone,

For the Gypsies ate him, flesh and bone."

By drao, also, they could avenge themselves on their enemies by destroying their cattle, without incurring a shadow of suspicion. Revenge for injuries, real or imaginary, is sweet to all unconverted minds—to no one more than the Gypsy, who, in all parts of the world, is, perhaps, the most revengeful of human beings.

But if the Gitános are addicted to any one superstition above others, it is in respect to the *loadstone*, to which they attribute all kinds of miraculous powers. They believe that he who is in possession of it has nothing to fear from steel or lead, from fire or water, and that death itself has no power over him. The Gypsy contrabandists are particularly anxious to procure this stone, which they carry upon their persons in their expeditions. They say, that in the event of their being pursued by the revenue officers, whirlwinds of dust will arise and conceal them from the view of their enemies; the horse stealers say much the same thing, and assert that they are uniformly successful when they bear about them the precious stone. But it is said by them to effect much more. It is extraordinary in exciting the amorous propensities, and on this account it is in great request among the Gypsy hags. All these women are procuresses, and find persons of both sexes weak and wicked enough to make use of their pretended knowledge in the composition of love draughts and decoctions.

In the Museum of Natural Curiosities at Madrid, there is a large piece of loadstone, originally extracted from the American mines. There is scarcely a Gitána in Madrid who is not acquainted with this circumstance, and who does not long to obtain the stone, or a part of it. Several attempts have been made to steal it, all of which, however, have been unsuccessful.

A translation of the Gospel of St. Luke was printed in the Gypsy language, at Madrid, in 1838. The chapters were read over and explained to some of these strange people, by the late agent of the British and Foreign Bible Society, in Spain. They said it was *lachō*, and *jucál*, and *mistō*, all of which words express approval of the quality of a thing; and they purchased copies of the Gypsy Luke freely. The women were particularly anxious to obtain copies, though unable to read; but each wished to have one in her pocket, especially when engaged in thieving expeditions, for they all looked upon it in the light of a charm, which would preserve them from all danger and mischance; some even went so far as to say, that in this respect it was equally as efficacious as the Bar Lachi, or loadstone, which they are generally so eager to possess. Of this Gospel, five hundred copies were printed, the greatest part of which were circulated among the Gypsies; but it was speedily prohibited by a royal ordinance, which appeared in the Gazette of Madrid, in August, 1838.

Before closing, under this head, we will remark that, although the Gypsies in general are a kind of wandering outcasts, incapable of appreciating the blessings of a settled and civilized life, yet among the Gypsies of Moscow there are not a few who inhabit stately houses, go abroad in elegant equipages, and are not a whit behind the higher order of Russians in appearance, nor in mental acquirements. To the female part of the Gypsy colony of Moscow is to be attributed the merit of this partial rise from abjectness and degradation, having from time immemorial so successfully cultivated the vocal art, that, though in the midst of a nation by whom song is more cherished and cultivated, and its principles better understood, than by any other of the civilized globe, the Gypsy choirs of Moscow are, by the general voice of the Russian public, admitted to be unrivalled in that most amiable of all accomplishments. It is a fact, notorious in Russia, that the celebrated Catalini was so enchanted with the voice of one of these Gypsy songsters, who, after the former had displayed her noble Italian talent before a splendid audience at Moscow, stepped forward, and with an astonishing burst of almost angelic melody, so enraptured every ear, that even applause forgot its duty, and the noble Catalini immediately tore from her own shoulders a shawl of Cashmere, which had been presented to her by the Father of Rome, and embracing the Gypsy, insisted on her acceptance of the splendid gift, saying, that it had been intended for the matchless songster which she now perceived she herself was not.

CHAPTER X.

OMENS, CHARMS, AND DIVINATION.

Many books have been published, having a tendency to deceive the credulous, who suffer themselves to be guided by any thing but reason and experience. Hence the encouragement bestowed on works of enchantment, dreams, omens, and fate. Mankind have always discovered a propensity to peep behind the veil of futurity, and have been lavish of money in consulting persons and books that make a pretension of unravelling the decrees of Fate, which lie hidden in the labyrinths of darkness. From these sources have arisen the following superstitions, as a sample of the many that have disturbed the peace of individuals, families, and sometimes of whole communities.

"A coal in the shape of a coffin, flying out of the fire to any particular person, denotes his death is not far off. A collection of tallow rising up against the wick of a candle is called a winding-sheet, and deemed an omen of mortality. If, in eating, you miss your mouth, and the food falls, it is very unlucky, and denotes sickness. To dream you are dressed in black is an unlucky omen. Some quarrel is about to happen between you and a friend or relative. Sickness is about to attend your family. Death will deprive you of some friend or relation. Lawsuits will perplex and harass you. If you undertake a journey, it will be unsuccessful. If you are in love, it denotes that your sweetheart is very unhappy, and that sickness will attend her. If you are a farmer, your crops will fail, the murrain will attack your cattle, and some dreadful accident will happen by the overturning of one of your wagons. If you are in business, some one will arrest you, and you will have great difficulty in settling the matter. To dream of hen and chickens is the forerunner of ill luck. Your sweetheart will betray you and marry another. If you go to law, the case will be decided against you. If you go to sea, you will lose your goods, and narrowly escape shipwreck. To dream of coals denotes much affliction and trouble. If you are in love, your sweetheart will prove false, and do every thing to injure you. To dream you see the coals extinguished, and reduced to cinders, denotes the death of yourself, or some near friend or relation. It also indicates great losses, and forewarns you of beggary and a prison. To dream you are married is ominous of death. It also denotes poverty, a prison, and misfortunes. To dream of lying with your newly-married husband or wife denotes danger and sudden misfortunes."

Popular charms are equally absurd and nonsensical. For example, a ring made of the hinge of a coffin is good for the cramp. A halter with which a man has been hanged, if tied about the head, will cure the headache. A drop of blood of a black cat cures convulsions in children. If a tree of any kind be split, and weak, rickety, or ruptured children are drawn through it, and afterwards the tree is bound together, so as to make it unite—as the tree heals and grows together, so will the child acquire strength. If in a family the youngest daughter be married before her older sisters, they must all dance at her wedding without shoes, to counteract their ill luck, and procure themselves husbands. And to procure luck when a person goes out to transact business, you must throw an old shoe after him. To spit on the first money received for the price of goods sold on any day will procure luck. And that boxers must spit in their hands before they set to, for luck's sake.

Seamen have a superstition that if they whistle in a storm, the storm will be increased. And in time of a calm, they practise whistling to *call the wind*, as they term it. Among farmers, in setting a hen, it is deemed lucky to use an odd number of eggs. Among soldiers, salutes with cannon must be of an odd number. A royal salute is thrice seven, or twenty-one guns. Healths are drank odd. Yet the number *thirteen* is sometimes deemed ominous; it being supposed that when thirteen persons meet in a room, one of them will die within the year. To know whether a woman shall have the man she desires, it is directed to get two lemon peels, and wear them all day, one in each pocket, and at night rub the four posts of the bedstead with them. If she is to succeed, the person will appear to her in her sleep, and present her with a couple of lemons. If not, there is no room for hope. And again the fair ones are directed to take a piece of wedding cake, draw it thrice through the wedding ring, lay it under their pillow, and they will certainly dream of their future husbands. A thousand other equally successful methods have been proposed to solve the mysteries of future fortune; and yet the magical stone, that will turn all our schemes into wished-for realities, remains to be discovered. As time advances, and knowledge pervades the abodes of darkness and ignorance, all this trumpery of ghosts, witches, fairies, tricks, and omens will go down to the "tomb of the Capulets." People will be able to pass through the churchyard, sleep in an old house, though the wind whistle ever so shrill, without encountering any supernatural visitations. They will become wise enough to trace private and public calamities to other causes than the crossing of knives, the click of an insect, or even the portentous advent of a comet. Thanks to the illustrious names recorded in the annals of science and letters, who have contributed towards so happy a consummation.

CHAPTER XI.

MODERN MIRACLES.

There are some who profess to believe in modern miracles. But such belief necessarily partakes of superstition. The Savior gave no intimation that miracles should continue after the establishment of Christianity. He promised to be with his apostles even unto the end of that age. He declared that all who believed their instructions should also have power to cast out devils, heal diseases, speak with new tongues, and withstand any deadly thing. But his promise did not extend beyond the immediate converts of the apostles. And we have no satisfactory evidence that miracles were wrought by any but these; while we have abundant testimony that our Savior's promise was literally fulfilled. In fact, there was no necessity for miracles after the establishment of Christianity. They were first wrought as so many testimonies that Jesus was the sent of God; and at the same time, were so many significant emblems of his designs, so many types and figures, aptly representing the benefits to be conferred upon the human race. But they were not designed to be perpetuated; for a history of divine revelation was committed to writing, and translated into the prevailing languages of the civilized world. If any could be so obstinate as not to be convinced of its divine origin by the mass of evidence with which it was accompanied, neither would they believe, though one should rise from the dead.

Pretended modern miracles admit of an easy explanation on natural principles. Diseases have been suddenly healed; but imagination effected the cure. Visions, ghosts, and apparitions have been seen; but they existed only in the minds of the observers, and were caused by some mental or bodily operation. But nothing of this kind can be said of the miracles of Christ. His cannot be accounted for on any natural principles, but must have been caused by divine miraculous agency.

Modern miracles are not supported by satisfactory evidence. They have been mostly wrought in secret. No witnesses can be produced but the most interested. This was not the case with those of our Savior. They were performed openly, and in the presence of friends and enemies. They could not be deceptions; for the resurrection of a dead person could be tested by the evidence of the senses. The remark of Judge Howe may be appropriately introduced in this connection. He had thoroughly and impartially studied the evidences of Christianity, and a firm belief in its divine origin was the result. He observed that no jury could be found that would give a verdict against Christianity, if the evidences on both sides could be fairly presented before them, and they were governed in forming their opinion by the common rules of belief. The truth of this observation is confirmed by the fact, that candid inquirers after truth have uniformly risen from an examination of the evidences of Christianity believers in its divine origin. The same cannot be said of modern miracles. No jury could be obtained of disinterested persons, who would give a verdict in their favor. Therefore we have no satisfactory evidence of their reality. Our safest course is to admit the conclusion of eminent writers of all denominations, namely, that miracles ceased with the first converts of Christianity.

CHAPTER XII.

PRETENDED PROPHETS AND CHRISTS.

Many have professed a belief in the divine inspiration of some one of the many false prophets or Christs that have appeared in different ages of the church. In the year 1830, there was a man in this country, calling himself Matthias, who declared that he was the very Christ, and pretended that he had come to judge the world. And strange as it may seem, he was attended by some individuals of quite respectable standing, who worshipped him as God! He appeared in pontifical robes, with his rule in his right hand, and his two-edged sword in the left. Underneath a rich olive broadcloth cloak, lined and faced with silk and velvet, he wore a brown frock coat, with several stars on each breast, and a splendid golden star on his left breast. His belt was of white cloth fastened by a golden clasp, surmounted by an eagle. He occasionally put on a cocked hat, of black beaver, trimmed with green, the rear angle being surmounted by the golden symbol of glory.

On being asked where his residence was, and what was his occupation, he replied, "I am a traveller, and my legal residence is Zion Hill, Westchester county, New York; I am a Jewish teacher and priest of the Most High, saying and doing all that I do, under oath, by virtue of my having subscribed to all the covenants that God hath made with man from the beginning up to this time. I am chief high priest of the Jews of the order of Melchizedec, being the last chosen of the twelve apostles, and the first in the resurrection which is at the end of 2300 years from the birth of Mahomet, which terminated in 1830, that being the summit of the power of the false prophets. I am now denouncing judgment on the Gentiles, and that judgment is to be executed in this age. All the blood from Zacharias till the death of the last witness is required of this generation. Before this generation passeth away, this judgment shall be executed and declared. The hour of God's judgment is come."

Matthias commenced his public career in Albany; but not making many converts there, he soon removed to the city of New York. Here he met with but little success for some time; but it appears that in the autumn of 1832, he had succeeded in ingratiating himself into the favor of a number of individuals, among whom were three of the most wealthy and respectable merchants of Pearl Street. He represented himself to them to be the Spirit of Truth, which had disappeared from the earth at the death of Matthias mentioned in the New Testament, and that the spirit of Jesus Christ entered into that Matthias whom he now represented, having risen again from the dead. This blasphemous impostor pretended to possess the spirit of Jesus of Nazareth, and that he now, at his second appearance of the spirit, was the Father, and had power to do all things, forgiving sins, and communicating the Holy Ghost to such as believed on him. And what was most astonishing and unparalleled, these men, who were before professors of the Christian religion, were blind enough to believe and confide in all he imposed on them.

So completely did he succeed in deluding these men, and in impressing them with the belief that he was actually a high priest of the order of the mysterious Melchizedec, upon a divine mission to establish the kingdom of God upon the earth, that he obtained entire control over them and their estates. "I know the end of all things," he would assert, illustrating it by placing a piece of paper in a drawer, leaving one end upon the outside, and saying, "You can see but one end of the paper, and so the world sees; but I see the whole length of it—I see the end."

Whenever he saw fit to call upon his dupes to contribute of their substance for his support and the promotion of the kingdom he was about to establish, he did so; and if they refused to provide him whatever money he desired, he threatened to visit upon them (which he declared he had the power to do) the wrath of the Almighty. But if they believed in him and obeyed him in all things, he promised them that they should be called into the kingdom, and he would forgive all their sins, and they should enjoy eternal happiness. Impudent and blasphemous as such language and pretensions truly were, the intended effect was produced, and the prophet received new encouragement by the gratification of pecuniary abundance. This object gained, he was enabled to adorn his person with costly apparel, and to obtain other appurtenances and furniture which he thought were necessary, that all things might correspond to the nature and dignity of the office which he had assumed.

In August, 1833, two of his friends and proselytes, Messrs. Pierson and Folger, were residing at Sing Sing, Westchester county. Thither, about that time, Matthias repaired, and took up his residence with Mr. Folger and family. In a week or two, Matthias came to the conclusion that their dwelling-place did not correspond with his character, and accordingly suggested to Folger and Pierson that it was their duty to hire, for his use, a house which he might consecrate wholly to himself. In this he was accommodated, not only without any hesitation, but with the acknowledgment that the request was reasonable. Soon after this, it appeared to Matthias's mind, that his habitation should not be subject to worldly interests or infidel intrusion; and he accordingly presumed to require of his two obedient followers the purchase of a house to be exclusively his own. With this request they agreed to comply. Before it was accomplished, however, Matthias manifested some new attribute of his character, and accompanied the revelation by an effort to make Folger believe that the house in which he then resided at Sing Sing, and had purchased some time previous for the use of himself and family, was purchased at the instigation of the Spirit of Truth, for him, Matthias— Folger having been the instrument under the influence of that Spirit for that purpose! So complete was Matthias's control, that Folger believed even this! And having resided with Messrs. Folger and Pierson about two months, he took *this* house, thus miraculously purchased, into his own especial charge. Matthias then required these gentlemen to give him an account of their property, and having obtained this statement, which exhibited their easy circumstances, he required both of them to enter into an agreement to support him, assuring them they should receive the blessing of God by so doing. This agreement was accordingly entered into, and Matthias enjoyed the full benefits of it for several months, when Mr. Folger became bankrupt. His wants were afterwards supplied by Pierson, until the death of Mr. P., which took place under very suspicious circumstances. It seems that a short time previous to this melancholy event, and while Mr. Pierson was yet in health, Matthias prevailed upon him to assign him his whole estate. And it seemed, by Matthias's account on his examination, that Messrs. Folger, Pierson, and Mills frequently declared to him that they believed him to be the *Father*, and that he was qualified to establish God's kingdom on earth, and that Zion Hill, which was the place miraculously purchased at Sing Sing, was transferred to him for that purpose, together with horses, carriages, and furniture of a house in Third Street, New York—that it was also agreed that the house and lot in Third Street should be conveyed to him, and that Mr. Pierson directed a deed to be made out accordingly, but died before it was completed. He still considered the property as his own for the original purpose, and considered it the beginning of the establishment of the kingdom. It is certain that Mr. Pierson was suddenly taken sick, and it was believed to be immediately after this contract was made. He fell under the care of Matthias, who would neither allow his friends to visit him, nor to call medical aid, declaring himself to "*have power of life and death.*" Mr. Pierson's body having been removed to New Jersey for interment, a post mortem examination was held by four respectable physicians, all of whom certified that they found in the stomach a "*large quantity of an unwholesome and deadly substance.*" Matthias was therefore arrested with the charge of having poisoned Mr. Pierson, on which he gave bail for appearance at court.

Soon after this, he went to the city of New York, and entering the family of Mr. Folger, resided with them for several months; but the mysterious death of Mr. Pierson, and the attending circumstances, having shaken the confidence of Mr. Folger and his family, they began to be conscious of their delusion, and resolved to abandon Matthias and his principles. On announcing their determination to him, he resorted to his old practice of threats and promises, and told them they must not throw him destitute on the world; that, if they did so, the blessing of God would depart from them, and sickness and perhaps death would follow; but if they gave him money to support him, the blessing of God should continue to them. Mr. Folger having become bankrupt, Matthias perhaps was willing to leave him—not, however, without having first insisted on a supply of money, which he obtained to the amount of six hundred and thirty dollars, and immediately left the city. On the morning of that day, Matthias partook of a very little breakfast, and scarcely tasted of the coffee, alleging, as an excuse, that he was ill. Immediately after breakfast, Mr. Folger, his wife, and children were taken sick. Mr. Folger did not suspect the cause of their illness, until after Matthias had left the city, when, upon examination, he learned that the black woman who did the cooking for the family had also abstained from the use of coffee that morning; and from other circumstances he became confirmed that the woman was bribed by Matthias to poison the family. The effort was unsuccessful, the poison producing but a temporary effect. This nefarious transaction induced Mr. Folger to procure the arrest of Matthias, firmly convinced, at this melancholy stage, that he was a *base impostor.*

The third gentleman named as one of the dupes of Matthias became a lunatic under the unfortunate delusion. But on a removal to the country, and from the influence of the "prophet," he recovered, and became convinced of his lamentable error.

In the sequel, it appeared that Matthias had received in the aggregate, from these gentlemen, about ten thousand dollars in money, and negotiable paper, which he appropriated in furnishing the establishment at Zion Hill and in Third Street. And by whatever means he obtained money, it is evident he used it for the wildest and most extravagant purposes. His wardrobe was most bountifully supplied with new boots, shoes, and pumps; linen shirts of the most exquisite fineness, the wristbands fringed with delicate lace; silk stockings, handkerchiefs, and gloves; coats embroidered with gold; merino morning dresses; and two caps made of linen cambric, folded in the form of a mitre, richly embroidered, one with the names of the twelve apostles written around it, and "Jesus Matthias" adorning the front in prominent characters, the other surrounded with the names of the twelve tribes, the front like the other. With his two-edged sword (with gold chain and mountings) he was to destroy the Gentiles, as Gideon did the Midianites. With his six feet rule he was to measure the New Jerusalem, "the gates thereof, and the walls thereof," and divide it into lots for those who believed on him, and obeyed the Spirit of Truth, as it came from him, the trumpet. With the golden key which he possessed, he was to unlock the gates of paradise.

Somewhat versed in the rites and antiquities of the Jews, this impostor united with a quick and active mind a considerable cunning, a fluent speech, and a vast amount of persevering impudence, and endeavored to impress his dogmas by assuming a sanctified and uncompromising air, and by invariably fixing upon his victim his remarkably fierce and penetrating eyes. He reasoned plausibly and ingeniously, and was exceedingly subtle at evasion. Although he never could have obtained an extensive and permanent influence, even if his knavery had not been detected, since his schemes were too wild and incoherent, and his demands too absurd to produce an effect that would endure beyond his actual and immediate presence, yet that his blasphemous pretensions should have gained any credence among intelligent minds is to be greatly lamented. The whole history of these transactions will form a dark page in the records of modern fanaticism, and will present an enduring but melancholy evidence of the weakness of human nature.

As an excuse for the conduct of Matthias, or Matthews, which was his real name, he was supposed by some to be laboring under monomania, partly hereditary and partly superinduced by religious fanaticism and frenzy. Still, he was not without "method in his madness;" and it seems evident that, with a tinge of insanity, he was also much of a knave, and probably a dupe in part to his own imposture. During his confinement in jail, awaiting his trial for the alleged murder of Mr. Pierson, Matthias issued a decree, commanding all the farmers to lay aside their ploughs, declaring, "As I live, there shall be no more sowing in the earth until I, the twelfth and last of the apostles, am delivered out of the house of bondage." He also prophesied that if he were convicted, White Plains should be destroyed by an earthquake, and not an inhabitant be left to tell the tale of its destruction; and strange to say, men were not found wanting who believed in his absurd and blasphemous predictions. On trial, the physicians who had examined the stomach of the deceased were led to suspect poison, but could not say positively that poison had been administered; whereupon the prisoner was discharged, on the ground that no evidence had been produced to convict him either of murder or manslaughter. In the case of his arrest at the instigation of Mr. Folger, that gentleman afterwards wrote to the district attorney, requesting him to dismiss the case, it not appearing to be an indictable one, and declaring, that the day—"so far as passing himself for a *pure* and *upright* man—has passed, and there is no danger of his imposing upon any one here or elsewhere." In a letter written by Mr. Folger, dated New York, Nov. 8, 1834, and published in the Commercial Advertiser, Mr. Folger says, "My object is now to rid myself of him and all connected with him, with as little trouble as possible. Mr. Pierson, myself, and family have been deeply, very deeply deluded, deceived, and imposed upon; and I regret exceedingly that the former could not have been spared to witness the deep deception. We are sensible of our error—we repent it sincerely; and although we cannot expect to recover, at present, the situation which we held in society previous to our acquaintance with this vile creature, yet in time we shall be able to show that we are enemies to him, and all who undertake to sustain him in his wickedness and plans to destroy us."

For closeness of resemblance, in many striking features, to the case of Matthias, was that of the Anabaptists of Munster, in Germany, which excited the wonder of Europe during the early part of the seventeenth century, and of which such strange accounts are to be found in the histories of that epoch. The similarity between the principal of this sect, known as John of Leyden, and Matthews, not only in doctrine, but in worldly observance, in the passion for magnificence of apparel and luxurious living, and in the rites and ceremonies exacted by each, is so remarkable as almost to lead to the conclusion that the latter had formed himself and his creed upon the model of his ancient prototype. The number of deluded proselytes who blindly followed the dictates of the Anabaptist leader was at one time so great, and their power so formidable, that several princes of Germany united against them; and it was not until after a vigorous siege, and an obstinate resistance, that the city of Munster, of which the fanatics had obtained complete possession, was taken and their power broken down.

This John of Leyden wore upon his head a triple crown of gold, richly adorned with gems. Around his neck he wore, suspended by a golden chain, an ornament of gold, representing the terrestrial globe, with a cross, and two swords, one of gold, the other of silver, with the inscription, "King of Righteousness over the whole world." He also assumed the title of "the Father," and he required all his followers to pledge themselves to do his will, and, if necessary, to suffer death at his command, or in his defence and service. He enjoined and enforced a community of goods, a surrender of all possessions, land, money, arms, and merchandise to him, as the Father and Lord of all, to be employed by him in the universal establishment of his kingdom; and he denounced the vengeance of Heaven and eternal damnation on all such as refused to believe in him and do his will. All churches and convents he commanded to be destroyed, the priests denounced as children of darkness, and all sovereigns he would put to death. He proclaimed the nullity of all marriages, except such as were solemnized by himself or his own prophets, but enjoined polygamy, himself setting the example. Each of his principal followers had from six to eight wives, and both men and women were compelled to marry. He taught that no man understood the Scriptures but himself, or those whom he enlightened with his spirit, and all the prophecies in the Old Testament, relating to the Savior, he applied to himself, and proclaimed their fulfilment in the establishment of his kingdom.

In our own country, the most surprising instance of imposture and delusion, perhaps, that has occurred, was that of the Cochranites, whose enormities in licentiousness made so much stir in Maine and New Hampshire a few years since. Cochrane was an officer in the army, thrown out of commission by the reduction of the military establishment of the United States, after the conclusion of the last war with England. Having become poor and penniless, he left Portland, and struck off into the country, seeking his fortune, and caring not whither he went. One day, as night drew on, he found himself near a farm house, weary and hungry, and without a penny to purchase a mouthful of food or the use of a pillow for the night. The thought struck him suddenly of throwing himself upon the hospitality of the farmer, for the occasion, in the character of a minister. Introducing himself as such to the family, he was cordially received, and as the country was new and destitute of clergymen, the good people forthwith despatched messengers to the neighbors, that a minister had come among them, and invited them in to attend a meeting. The impostor had not anticipated so speedy a trial of his clerical character; but having assumed it, there was no escape—he must act the part, for the time being, in the best way he could. Being neither ignorant nor destitute of talents, he succeeded in acquitting himself much better than he had anticipated, and gave so much satisfaction to his audience as to induce him to persevere in the imposture he had commenced. As he acquired skill and confidence by practice in his new vocation, his popularity increased, and he soon found it a profitable occupation. He was followed by multitudes, and it was not long before he announced himself as some great one, and founded a new sect of religionists. His command over the audiences which he addressed is said to have been wonderful, and his influence over his followers unbounded. It seemed as though he was enabled to hold the victims of his impostures in a state of enchantment. A professor in an eastern college having heard of the wonderful sway which Cochrane held over his disciples, and of the impressions he made upon casual hearers, determined one evening to go and witness his performances. While present, although a very cool and grave personage, he said he felt some strange, undefinable, mysterious influence creeping over him to such a degree, that he was obliged actually to tear himself away, in apprehension of the consequences. This gentleman, however, was a believer in animal magnetism, and was therefore inclined to attribute it to that cause. It was said that if the impostor did but touch the hand or neck of a female, his power over her person and reason was complete. Consequently it led to the most open and loathsome sensuality.

So atrocious was his conduct, that he seduced great numbers of females, married and unmarried, under the pretext of raising up a holy race of men. The peace of many families was broken up, and the village kept an establishment like a seraglio—a disgusting and melancholy commentary upon the weakness of human nature. His career, however, was but of short duration.

A history of religious impostures would form a library of itself. The human mind, in all ages and countries, and under all forms of government and religion, seems to have been wonderfully susceptible of delusion and imposition upon that subject, which, of all others, is the most important for time and eternity. The court of Egypt was deluded by the impostors who undertook to contend with Moses. And the chosen people themselves, notwithstanding the direct disclosures which the Most High had made of himself, in all their wonderful history, were prone to turn aside from the worship of the true God, to follow the lying spirits of the prophets of Baal and other deceivers, from the days of Moses till the destruction of Jerusalem. So, likewise, under the Christian dispensation, from the defection of Simon Magus to the wild delirium of Edward Irving, there have been a succession of Antichrists, until their name is legion— pretenders to divine missions, the power of working miracles, the gift of tongues—perverting the Scriptures, leading astray silly men and women— destroying the peace of families, throwing communities into confusion, and firebrands into the church—clouding the understandings, and blinding the moral perceptions of men, and subverting the faith of these even whose mountains stood strong, and who had been counted among the chosen people of God. "In the last days," says the apostle Peter, "there shall come scoffers, walking after their own lusts,"—"chiefly them which walk after the flesh, in the lust of uncleanness, and despise government; presumptuous are they, self-willed; they are not afraid to speak evil of dignities; sporting themselves in their own deceivings, having eyes full of adultery, and that cannot cease from sin; beguiling unstable souls; for when they speak great swelling words of vanity, they allure through the flesh, through much wantonness, those that were clean escaped from them who live in error; while they promise them liberty, they themselves are the servants of corruption." Jude also admonishes us "to remember that they were foretold as mockers, who should be in the last time, who should walk after their own ungodly lusts. These be they who separate themselves, sensual, not having the Spirit."

It is wonderful to observe with what precision these prophecies have been fulfilled by the clouds of impostors who have appeared—"spoken great swollen words of vanity," and fallen—since the inspired sentences were uttered. And it may be regarded as one of the evidences of the truth of inspiration, that, had the long array of apostates and deceivers actually stood before the sacred penmen, at the time of their writing, their characters all naked before them, the likenesses, from the first Christian apostate to the sensual Mormons, could not have been drawn with greater fidelity. The "TRUTH OF GOD," distinctly set forth in the book of Revelation, is an infallible criterion by which to test the true character of any religious opinion or practice; nor can any radical or fundamental error long escape detection, when subjected to this plain and unerring standard.

CHAPTER XIII.

MORMON SUPERSTITION.

A certain Joseph Smith, Jr., pretended, a few years ago, to have been directed by the Spirit of God to dig, in a hill, in the township of Manchester, Ontario county, New York, for a set of golden plates which were there concealed, and upon which were inscribed sacred records by the hands of Mormon. He obeyed the direction and found the plates. The inscriptions upon them were in an unknown tongue. But, by the special power of the Spirit, Smith was enabled to translate them. A volume containing these writings was soon after published, constituting, in the whole, fifteen books, purporting to have been written at different times, and by the different authors whose names they respectively bear. In these writings there seems to be a bungling attempt to imitate the style of the sacred Scriptures. But the attempt is manifestly unsuccessful. Nearly two thirds of the paragraphs are introduced with the phrase, "And it came to pass." In endeavoring to preserve the solemn style of the Scriptures, there is great disregard of grammatical propriety. We read, "The Lord *sayeth* unto me, and I *sayeth* unto the Lord." Perhaps a few extracts, selected at chance, will give the reader a more correct idea of the general style of the book than any remarks we might offer.

"And it came to pass that when they had *arriven* in the borders of the land of the Lamanites."

"And it came to pass that I Nephi did make *bellowses* wherewith to blow the fire."

"And it came to pass that Limhi and many of his people *was* desirous to be baptized."

The Mormon preachers claim for themselves and the members of their church the power of working miracles, and of speaking with new tongues. They jabber with some strange sounds, and call this the speaking with tongues. They assert it as a fact, that among them the dead have been raised, and the sick healed, as in the days of Christ and his apostles. From these *facts*, as they call them, they draw the conclusion that *they* are the members of the true church of Christ. The doctrine increases among men; and well it may, for there are circumstances in the condition and views of those who embrace it which are calculated to secure its success. In a large portion of the community there is a great degree of ignorance in regard to the geography of the sacred Scriptures, the manners and customs of the

Jews, and the natural history of the Bible. There are many who read their Bibles daily, and with true devotional feelings, it may be, who have no idea that the places mentioned in sacred history, like those mentioned in any other history, can be traced on the map, can be found and visited at the present day, although disguised under modern names. It makes no part of their study of the Bible to ascertain where the places mentioned are to be found, and what they are now called. They have no idea that the allusions to manners and customs, found in the Bible, can be understood, through an acquaintance with the practices and habits of the people described; and, consequently, the study of Jewish manners and customs makes no part of their preparation for understanding the Scriptures. They have no idea that the allusion in Scripture to facts in natural history can be verified by an acquaintance with that science, and therefore they make no exertions to understand the natural history of the Bible. They do not take up the Bible and read it with the expectation of being able to understand it, in regard to these particulars, as they would understand any other book. All such are prepared, by their ignorance on these subjects, to become the dupes of the Mormon delusion; or, at least, they are not prepared to withstand this delusion. They open the Book of Mormon, claiming to be a kind of appendix to the Bible. The paragraphs begin with the phrase, "And behold it came to pass." They read of the cities of Zarahemla, Gid, Mulek, Corianton, and a multitude of others. They read of prophets and preachers, of faith, repentance, and obedience; and having been accustomed, in reading the Scriptures, to take all such things just as they are presented, without careful examination, they can see no reason why all this is not as much entitled to belief as are the records of the Old and New Testaments. But if, on the contrary, they were acquainted with the geography and the natural history of the Bible, and with the manners and customs of the nations there mentioned, and especially if, in their reading of the Scriptures, they were accustomed to examine carefully into these points, they would at once perceive the utter impossibility of identifying the cities mentioned in the Book of Mormon with any geographical traces which they can now make. They would thus perceive the deception, and be put on their guard. And then, too, upon further examination, they would discover that the manners and customs of the people, the sentiments and disputes, are not such as belong to the period of the world in which the people are represented to have lived; that they take their coloring from modern customs, from modern opinions and controversies; and, upon these discoveries, they would be led to reject the whole as a fabrication.

Many are deceived in consequence of the fluency of the preachers in warning sinners. They pray with fervor; the people are affected; and the Spirit of God is declared to be present, owning and blessing the work. But there is deception here. It is but a few years since the Cochrane delusion, as it is called, prevailed in and around the village of Saco, Maine. What gave that delusion so much success? It was because Cochrane spoke with great fluency, warned sinners with great earnestness, and poured forth his prayers with zealous fervor. The people became affected; many were in tears; many sobbed aloud, cried for mercy, and some became prostrate on the floor. "Surely," it was remarked, "the doctrines advanced by Cochrane must be true, the preaching of them being so signally owned and blessed of God." In this way, men of sound judgment in other respects are carried away by false views and appearances, and become the dupes of the most extravagant sentiments and delusions. They become "zealously affected," but it is not, as the apostle says, "in a good thing." A correct knowledge of the sacred Scriptures, and of proper principles in regard to the study of the Bible, with sound and rational views of the nature of religion, and of the influences of the Holy Spirit, will serve to correct all such tendencies to error and deception.

From the best account that has been published respecting the *origin* of the Mormon Bible, it appears that it was written by an individual named Solomon Spaulding, some twenty-five years ago; but without the least intention, on the part of the author, of framing a system of delusion for his fellow-men. This Spaulding was a native of Ashford, in Connecticut, where he was distinguished, at an early age, for his devotion to study, and for the superiority of his success over that of his schoolmates. He received an academic education, and commenced the study of law at Windham; but his mind inclining to religious subjects, he abandoned the law, went to Dartmouth College, prepared himself for the ministry, and was regularly ordained. For some reasons unknown he soon abandoned that profession, and established himself as a merchant at Cherry Valley, New York. Failing in trade, he removed to Conneaut, in Ohio, where he built a forge; but again failed, and was reduced to great poverty. While in this condition, he endeavored to turn his education to account, by writing a book, the sale of which he hoped would enable him to pay his debts and support his family. The subject selected by him was one well suited to his religious education. It was an historical novel, containing an account of the aborigines of America, who were supposed by some to have descended from the ten tribes of Israel. The work was entitled the "Manuscript Found," and the history commenced with one Lehi, who lived in the reign of Zedekiah, king of Judea, six hundred years before the Christian era. Lehi, being warned of Heaven of the dreadful calamities that were impending over Jerusalem, abandoned his possessions, and fled with his family to the wilderness. After wandering for some time, they arrived at the Red Sea, and embarked on board a vessel. In this, after floating about for a long time, they reached America, and landed at the Isthmus of Darien. From the different branches of this family were made to spring all the Indian nations of this continent.

From time to time they rose to high degrees of civilization and refinement; but desolating wars among themselves scattered and degraded them. The Manuscript was written in the style of the Bible, the old English style of James the First. When the work was ready for the press, Spaulding endeavored to obtain the pecuniary assistance necessary for its publication, but his affairs were in so low a condition that he could not succeed. He then removed to Pittsburg, and afterwards to Amity, in Pennsylvania, where he died. By some means or other, the Manuscript fell into the hands of Joseph Smith, Jr., who afterwards published it under the name of the "Golden Bible." Smith was the son of very poor and superstitious parents, and was for a long time engaged in digging for Kidd's money, and other feats of like description. Possessing considerable shrewdness, he became somewhat skilled in feats of necromancy and juggling. He had the address to collect about him a gang of idle and credulous young men, whom he employed in digging for hidden treasures. It is pretended that, in one of the excavations they made, the mysterious plates from which the Golden Bible was copied were found. Such, briefly is the origin of the Mormon faith—a humbug to which not a few, otherwise sensible men, have pinned their hopes of happiness here and hereafter.

After the death of Joseph Smith, and shortly before the Mormons were driven out from Illinois, many of the disciples of the great impostor seceded and refused to acknowledge the leadership of the knowing twelve who became his successors. Among them were a very pious Mormon named McGhee Vanduzen, and his wife Maria. They soon gave to the world an exposition of the shameful manœuvres attendant upon Mormonism as a religion; of the absurd and indecent ceremonies which the unprincipled leaders of that wicked imposture enforced upon their infatuated disciples. Smith, and his associate leaders at Nauvoo, evidently established these ceremonies for the base purpose of enticing the more beautiful females among his disciples to their ruin and disgrace. The shameful character of the mysteries developed could lead to no other conclusion.

Says the Boston Traveller, of April 21, 1852, "The rapid spread of Mormonism is one of the mysteries of the age. A more barefaced delusion, except that of the spiritual rappings, was never imposed on the all-swallowing credulity of mankind. Yet it has gained adherents by thousands in Europe as well as in the United States."

CHAPTER XIV.

MILLER DELUSION.

A man by the name of William Miller published a book in the year 1836, in which he undertook to show that this earth would be destroyed in the year 1843. His calculation, as to the transpiration of such an event during the said year, is founded upon the prophecy of Daniel, that the *sanctuary should be cleansed!* in two thousand three hundred days. He took the days to mean years, and began his reckoning from the going forth of the commandment to restore Jerusalem, mentioned in a subsequent vision. Why did he not begin the reckoning from the date of the vision itself? Because this would not answer Mr. Miller's turn. To tell the people that the earth was to be burned up in 1747, would produce little or no excitement. He must hit upon a time for the beginning which would make the end yet future, in order to gratify his love for the marvellous.

That Mr. Miller intended to manage his reckoning of time to suit his own scheme, is obvious from his different computations of time, to *make* his interpretations of other prophecies comport with his application of the two thousand three hundred days. Daniel says, "And from the time that the daily sacrifice shall be taken away, and the abomination that maketh desolate set up, there shall be a thousand two hundred and ninety days." "Blessed is he that waiteth, and cometh to the thousand three hundred and five and thirty days." Taking the thousand three hundred and thirty-five days to reach from the taking away of the daily sacrifice, and setting up the abomination that maketh desolate, to the resurrection, he subtracts the thousand three hundred and thirty-five from it, and finds the remainder to be five hundred and eight, which must, to suit his calculation, be the year of our Lord in which the daily sacrifice should be taken away, &c. Then, to get at the taking away of a daily sacrifice, and the setting up of an abomination that maketh desolate, which should come any where in the neighborhood of this date, he makes the taking away of the daily sacrifice to be the doing away of the pagan worship in Rome, and the setting up the abomination spoken of to be the commencement of the Papal authority. This he sets at A.D. 508, without reference to fact, because his reckoning of prophetic time brings it so. The truth is, that the pagan character of Rome ceased soon after the conversion of the Emperor Constantine to Christianity, which was about A.D. 313. This makes about 195 years' difference in the age of the world, and brings it to an end in 1648, over 200 years ago!

But let us examine a little farther. Having come, as we have shown, at A.D. 508, which, having taken from the years of Christ's life 33, leaves 475 from the death of Christ, he proceeds to add up: The 70 weeks, or 490 years, to the crucifixion of Christ, 490; from the crucifixion of Christ to the taking away the daily sacrifice, 475. And here are his time, times, and half, which he takes to be the duration of the pagan reign, i.e., three years and a half, which, taking a day for a year, makes 1260.

Here, then, he has his whole time, down to the end of his second or Papal transgression of desolation, which he has all along held to be the end of the world. But these several numbers added amount to but 2225, 75 short of the 2300, reckoning from the going forth of the decree to rebuild Jerusalem. And what now shall be done? How shall the 75 years be made up to bring the end of the world to 1843? Why, he succeeds in finding two different numbers in the 12th of Daniel, viz., 1290 and 1335. And nothing is easier, when you have two different numbers, to substract the less from the greater. This he does in the present case, and finds the difference to be just 45. Well, what of that? Why, he says this is the time which was to elapse between the destruction of the great beast in his second or Papal character, and the resurrection! He does not pretend that the vision mentions this, but so he fixes it. He is like a country schoolmaster, who, not always finding it easy to manage by rules, when a scholar would carry him a sum which he could not work, he would look at the answer in the book, and get the difference between that and his own, and then he would slip in the ascertained difference, somewhere in the operation, to be added or substracted, as the case might require, to bring the answer as he wished it.

But although he succeeded in finding 45 years, he is still minus 30, for it brings out the end in 1813. And how shall the other 30 years be found? It must be gotten somehow, for who will believe it as it now stands? Yet this extraordinary man meets with no difficulty in finding the 30 years. In his parade of parts, of factors, to make up the great whole, he sets down for the space between the putting down of the Pagan power, to the setting up the same power, 30 years! And how he gets this number there, no mortal can tell. Yes, he tells us himself.

Considering himself so great a prophet, he seems to think that his own suppositions will certainly pass among others as good authority. He therefore unblushingly tells us that he *supposes* this 30 years. Hear him, (page 96.) "Therefore, to reconcile these two statements, *we must conclude* there were 30 years from A.D. 508, when paganism ceased, before the image beast, or Papal Rome, would begin her reign. *If* this is correct, then," &c.

Here, then, the foundation on which he keeps the world standing from 1813 to 1843, is a simple *if.* And to get in these supposititious 30 years, between the death of the pagan and the life of the Papal beast, he involves himself in a maze of absurdity. He makes the taking away of the daily sacrifice to be the putting an end to the Papal beast, that did daily sacrifice to idol abominations. The little horn, by whom the daily sacrifice was taken away, Mr. Miller takes to be the Papal beast, or Catholic church. This beast takes away the daily sacrifice, i.e., puts an end to the pagan beast, and yet does not exist until 30 years after the pagan beast is dead. This is truly an unheard of strait for a schemer to come to, to be obliged, in order to bring out his reckoning, to get 30 years between the existence of two beasts, one of which kills the other. The second beast slays the first, and performs many wonderful works, 30 years before he has any existence! No marvel that the man who could see into such mysteries should imagine that he could see the end of the world in 1843!

Mr. Miller commits various other errors in his calculations and dates, as, for instance, he states that pagan Rome commenced 148 years before Christ, whereas Rome was founded by Romulus, as an independent government, 752 years before Christ, being pagan from its beginning. He dates the erection of the Papal authority at A.D. 538. By the Papal power he means, of course,—not the Papal doctrine, for that existed much earlier than 538,—but the establishment of the civil authority. And this was not until about A.D. 750.

Indeed, Mr. Miller is palpably wrong in nearly all his positions; and the reason is, he is not looking for facts, but for reckonings to fill out his own scheme. And even in this, too, he fails. On page 109 of his Course of Lectures, first published in 1836, speaking of events to happen in 1839, he holds the following language: "He that is filthy will be filthy still. Mankind will, for a short season, give loose to all the corrupt passions of the human heart. No laws, human or divine, will be regarded; all authority will be trampled under foot; anarchy will be the order of government, and confusion *fill the world with horror and despair.* Murder, treason, and crime will be *common law,* and division and disunion *the only bond of fellowship.* Christians will be persecuted unto death, and dens and caves of the earth will be their retreat. *All things* which are not *eternal* will be *shaken to pieces,* that which cannot be shaken may remain. And this, if I am right in my calculations, will begin *on or before* A.D. 1839. 'And at *that time* (1839) thy people shall be delivered, every one that shall be found written in the book.' *Now* is come salvation indeed. The people of God are *now* to be delivered from outward foes and inbred lusts, from the corruptions of the grave and the vileness of the flesh. Every one, the poor and despised child of God, will *then* (in 1839) be delivered when he makes up his jewels.'"

Mr. Miller, in finding that things did not take place as he prophesied, put a note in the end of his book, on the last page, stating that he had made a *mistake of one year* in some of his computations, and hence these things which he *supposed* would take place in 1839, according to the first computation, will not be realized until the year 1840! And yet 1840 passed over our heads, and these things did not take place. On page 296 of his Lectures, he says the sixth vial was poured out in 1822, when the Ottoman power began to be dried up. This he considered to be a very important sign, indicating that we were on the very brink of the *judgment day*. Here he introduces Rev. xvi. 12. "And the sixth angel poured out his vial upon the great River Euphrates; and the waters thereof were dried up, that the way of the kings of the earth might be prepared." This preparation, Mr. M. says, is for the last great battle, which will take place at the pouring out of the seventh vial, in the year 1839 or 1840. "At the pouring out of the seventh vial, a voice from the throne will pronounce the words, *It is done*. The kingdoms of the earth and the governments of the world will be carried away, and their places be known no more." But these kingdoms still remain.

Mr. Miller's last assumption was, that Christ would come in the spring of 1844, at the date corresponding with the ending of the Jewish year for 43. Mr. M. says, in his preface to his book, "If I have erred in my exposition of the prophecies, *the time, being so near at hand*, will soon expose my folly." He had already seen the folly of some of his computations, and he seemed to fear lest it might prove the same in the final result also. And this he soon experienced, as may be seen by reading his *confession*, made at the Tabernacle in Boston, on the evening of May 28, 1844. He there stated that what he had preached and published respecting the coming of the Lord in 1843 was done honestly; (!) that he fully believed it; but that the time had now *passed*, and he was *proved to be mistaken*; that when the time arrived and the event did not take place, he felt bad—felt lonely—thought he should never have any more to say in public; that he felt worse on the account of others than he did for himself. He said there was an error somewhere in his calculations, but he could not tell where. He had now no definite time—he should wait God's time: it might come in a day, it might not come in fifty years; he could not say exactly when; he was waiting. Thus the whole affair exploded—came to nought; although much evil in regard to Mr. Miller's prophecies may yet be experienced in the community. Some will yet cling most obstinately to the system, and still maintain that Christ may be expected every day, hour, or minute, while others will fix upon some other date within a short period of time. They will still refer us to certain signs in the starry heavens, endeavoring to persuade the people to believe that the whole machinery of nature is out of joint, and that this is a certain precursor to the speedy dissolution of the world.

One of the second advent preachers gave the startling intelligence that *"fifteen hundred* stars had *recently* faded from the vault of heaven." But what are the facts? Not more than *thirteen* stars are recorded in the annals of astronomy as having been lost; and so far from having faded *recently*, some of them disappeared many ages since. It is not even certain that any stars have been blotted out. There are nearly one hundred variable stars which have periods of unusual brilliancy, and then gradually fade till nearly invisible, and after a time revive again. The thirteen missing stars may be of this description. These changes were observed many centuries ago. The bright star which appeared suddenly, with unusual splendor and brilliancy, in Cassiopeia, in 1572, is supposed to be the same star which suddenly appeared in the same place, with great lustre, about the year 900, and also about 600 years before, during the intervals of which it was invisible.

The same preacher adduced the Aurora Borealis as another sign of the last days. "Is it not remarkable," says he, "that no record of them appears till *quite recently*?" But what are the facts? It was indeed supposed by many, who had not investigated the subject, that the Aurora was first seen in England in 1716; but on examination we find it spoken of in 1560, in a scientific work, entitled A Description of Meteors, published soon after the invention of printing, subsequent to which, and before 1716, there are many accounts of the same phenomenon.

Many have supposed that nothing has ever before appeared, similar to the remarkable *red Aurora*, which was witnessed on the evening of January 25, 1837. Yet such spectacles have often been witnessed in the northern parts of Sweden, Lapland, and Siberia, and in remote and different periods. The Aurora is a great blessing in those high northern latitudes, where the sun is absent for many weeks, furnishing the inhabitants with a splendid light, in the midst of their dreary winter nights. Gmelin describes the Aurora Borealis of those regions as differing in color according to the states of the atmosphere, "sometimes assuming the appearance of blood." He observes that "they frequently begin with single bright pillars rising in the north, and almost at the same time in the north-east, which, gradually increasing, comprehend a large space in the heavens, rush about, with incredible velocity, from place to place, and finally almost cover the whole sky to the zenith, producing an appearance as if a vast tent was expanded in the heavens, glittering with gold, rubies, and sapphire. A more beautiful spectacle cannot be painted." These lights occasionally come so far south as to illuminate the sky in our latitude. Sometimes they have not appeared for many years. In 1716, these lights were seen in England, though never witnessed before by the oldest inhabitants living; and, as might be expected, they were alarmed, and actually supposed the day of judgment had come. From Barber's History of New England, we learn that the first appearance of the northern lights in this country, after the period of its first settlement, was on December 11, 1719, "when they were remarkably bright; and, as people in general had never heard of such a phenomenon, they were extremely alarmed with the apprehension of the final judgment. All amusements, all business, and even sleep was interrupted, for want of a little knowledge of history." We were told by some of the advent preachers that meteors and shooting stars, falling to the earth, were never seen until 1799. But this is a great mistake. As early as the year 472, Theophanes relates, "The sky appeared to be on fire, with the coruscations of flying meteors." Virgil, in his book of Georgics, speaks as follows:—

"And oft, before tempestuous winds arise,

The seeming *stars fall headlong* from the skies,

And, *shooting* through the darkness, gild the night

With sweeping glories and *long trails of light*."

In 553, under the reign of Justinian, were seen showers of falling stars in extraordinary numbers. In 763, under that of Constantine Capronymus, the same spectacle was witnessed. In 1099, in the month of November, it is said, in Vogel's Leipzig Chronicles, that there was seen an unheard-of number of falling stars, burning torches, and fiery darts in the sky. In 1464, on the 7th of November, the great meteoric stone fell at Ensisheim, in Alsace. On the 8th of August, 1723, numerous falling stars appeared in · many parts of the heavens, like fireflies.

But we are told of the sun and moon appearing like blood, and that this sign of our Lord's second coming was never witnessed, since the resurrection, till the year 1780. Yet this is likewise a mistake; for in the Basle Chronicle of Urtisus, under the year 1566, mention is made of the fact, that on the 28th and 29th of July, the sun and moon became *blood red*; and on the 7th of August, this striking phenomenon was again repeated. And, according to the Frankfort Chronicle of Lersner, under the year 1575, on the 29th of July, a *remarkable redness of the sun* occurred.

It has been said that the *darkness* of the sun, that occurred in 1780, was a sign given to portend the speedy destruction of the world. Why was it not then witnessed simultaneously in all parts of the earth? It was confined principally to New England and witnessed only by the generation preceding the present. To be sure, thousands were appalled by the event, and a feeling that the judgment day had actually come rested upon many minds. But yet they were in a mistake. This darkness commenced on the 19th of May, between the hours of 10 and 11 A.M., and continued until the middle of the next night. Persons were unable to read common print, determine the time of day by their clocks or watches, dine, or manage their business, without additional light. Candles were lighted in their houses. The birds sang their evening songs, disappeared, and became silent. The fowls retired to roost. The cocks were crowing all around, as at break of day. Objects could be distinguished but at a very little distance, and every thing bore the appearance and gloom of night. The legislature of Connecticut was in session at this time, in Hartford city. A very general opinion prevailed that the judgment day was at hand. The House of Representatives, being unable to transact business, adjourned. A proposal to adjourn the council was under consideration. When the opinion of Colonel Davenport was asked, he answered, "I am against an adjournment. The day of judgment is either approaching, or it is not. If it is not, there is no cause for an adjournment; if it is, I choose to be found doing my duty. I wish, therefore, that candles may be brought."

A similar darkness has sometimes gathered over the city of London, in consequence of a vast accumulation of smoke, so as to make it necessary for passengers in the streets to use lighted torches at midday. In 1783, a great part of Europe was for weeks overspread with a haziness of atmosphere which caused great consternation. The churches were crowded with supplicants. The astronomer Lalande attempted to allay the fright by endeavoring to account for the appearance, which he ascribed to an uncommon exhalation of watery particles from the great rain of the preceding year. But at last it was ascertained to be owing to smoke, occasioned by the great eruption of the volcano Hecla, which covered more than three thousand square miles with burning lava, in some places to the depth of forty feet. Dr. Franklin was in Europe at the time, and afterwards gave an account of the circumstances relating to this uncommon eruption. In fact, immense issues of smoke, from fires and volcanoes, have, from time immemorial, produced similar effects in different countries.

We will subjoin a few remarkable appearances that have taken place in the heavens, that the reader may at once perceive that in scarcely any age of the world have its inhabitants been destitute of some *sign*, that might, to the timid and uninformed, be considered as the prognostication of some awful catastrophe about to happen.

In 1574, on the 15th of November, *large and terrific beams of fiery light* were seen during the night. And similar appearances are noted in Vogel's Chronicles, as having occurred in November, 1637, and 1661. In the old Breslau Collections, there is mention made of a large *moonlike meteor*, which passed off with an explosion, on the 10th of November, 1721; and of a great *fire-flash*, or *flame-emitting comet*, on the 12th day. According to Vogel's Chronicles, there appeared on the 30th November, 1663, *a large cross*, and other signs in the skies. On the 11th of August, 1561, there was seen, in the forenoon, *a very remarkable red meteor*, emitting frequent *flashes of light*. In 1717, *numerous meteors* were seen at Fryeburg; and at Utchland, in August, 1715. On the 10th of August, 1717, *a large fire-ball* was seen in Lusace, Silesia, Poland, and Hungary. In the Frankfort Chronicle of July 29, 1694, it is mentioned that *the heavens were full of fiery flames!* as also again on the 9th of August. On February 22, 1719, *a large fire-ball* was seen in several places. On the 22d, 1720, *an immense red cross* was seen at Novogorod and Kiew; and on the 19th, 1722, *a huge fire-ball!*

What would the Millerites think, if they should now see "an immense red cross in the heavens," "a remarkable red meteor, emitting flashes of light during the night," or "a blood-red appearance of the sun and moon," and "showers of falling stars in extraordinary numbers"? These things are as likely to happen at the present day as they were a hundred years ago, and still the world remains as it has remained.

Just before the last return of Halley's comet, an article was published in a religious paper in this state, going to show that the world would probably be struck and set on fire by a comet, and that, most likely, Halley's would be the one to do it, as it was coming much nearer the earth than it had ever been before. The editor seemed to be ignorant that the quantity of matter that enters into the constitution of a comet is exceedingly small, and that the comet of 1770, which was quite large and bright, passed through the midst of Jupiter's satellites without deranging their motions in the least perceptible degree. Comets, it is believed, consist of exceedingly rare vapor; indeed, so much so, that some philosophers say that our thinnest clouds are dense in comparison. And yet this exceedingly thin vapor was to dash the world to atoms, or set it on fire, it was not fully determined which.

Whether comets, or any unusual appearances in the sky, are to be considered as *signs* prognosticating the final dissolution of all things, as being near at hand, is for each to determine for himself. And in forming a judgment upon the subject, we may surely be permitted to exercise the common sense which God has given us. To lay this aside, and judge only by *feeling* or *fancy*, is to criminally reject a light which we are *sure* is from God, and follow one which *may* prove an *ignis fatuus*, and land us in the quagmire of infidelity. If the Scripture signs are to receive a *literal* fulfilment, we may reasonably expect that they will conform to the four following tests:—

1. They will appear *near* the event of which they are intended as the harbinger; probably within the generation of those who will be living at the end of the world.

2. They will be witnessed in all parts of the earth, because all are alike interested.

3. They may *all* be expected to appear, and not a single class of phenomena without the other.

4. They will be such as will impress intelligent minds with their strangeness and peculiarity.

The Aurora Borealis conforms not to any of these tests. It has been seen for centuries, and is confined to the northern portions of the globe; having rarely, if ever, been seen so far north as the thirtieth degree of north latitude. And, as we have before remarked, the darkness of 1780 was confined principally to New England. And from a careful examination of all the accounts we have been able to collect of meteoric showers of the last and present century, the whole of them together have occupied a space on the globe less than one eighth of its surface. The shower of 1799 was probably the most extensive. Its centre was near the middle of the Atlantic; its edges touched the northern parts of South America, the coast of Labrador and Greenland, and the western shores of Europe and Africa. That of 1833 may be represented on a six-inch globe by the space occupied by a dollar. Such magnificent scenes are calculated to impress the mind with awe; yet it is surprising that many intelligent persons should suppose them to be the precursors of the final conflagration. If the simple but reasonable tests we have given be correct, they are disarmed of their character as ominous of the destruction of the world.

With regard to any changes in the order or succession of the heavenly bodies, it is only necessary to observe, that hundreds of scientific men, in Europe and America, have for many years been employed in exploring the material heavens with the most powerful telescopes. Many are employed, by the governments of Europe, in astronomical observations, scattered over the earth, for the express purpose of making new discoveries, if possible, and of furthering the interests of science. No phenomenon escapes their notice; and should any thing extraordinary occur, it would appear before the public, vouched by names that would command universal credence. It may be unnecessary to add, that no such changes in the planets and fixed stars, as have been proclaimed to the world by some of the second advent preachers, have been observed by learned astronomers and men of science.

CHAPTER XV.

INTERCOURSE WITH DEPARTED SPIRITS.

In no age, says a popular writer, has the world been destitute of those who professed, by some instrumentality or other, to hold intercourse with departed spirits. Neither has any age been without its reputed spectres, ghosts, or apparitions. The high priest of the Buddhist and Hindoo temples, in former times, when arrayed in the consecrated garments for the festivals, wore a round knob, about the size of a large pendent drop of a chandelier, suspended from his neck by a chain of great value and of dazzling brilliancy. It was through the agency of this crystal that he was supposed to hold communion with the spirit or spirits to whom he and his followers accorded devotion and made intercessions; and the glass, acting as did the famed oracle of Delphi, gave orders and commands, and settled all great questions that might be submitted to its spiritual master. The priest, although he might be a pattern of purity, and the quintessence of all that was good, having, however, the sin of being in years, and not able, perhaps, to hide from the spirit inhabiting the crystal all the transactions of his youth, could not hold a direct communication with it. To arrange this, a certain number of boys, and sometimes, in some of the temples, young damsels, were retained, who, having never mixed with the world, could not be supposed to be in any way contaminated by its vices. These alone were said to be capable of beholding the spirit when he chose to make his appearance in the divining glass, and interpreting to and fro the questions put and answers received. Although it was not every boy or *seer* to whom was permitted the gift of spiritual vision, yet in latter times, when divining crystals multiplied, little ragged boys would run after the passers in the streets, and offer to *see* any thing that might be required of them, for a trifling gift, even a cake or sweetmeat. In Egypt, the divining glass is superseded by putting a blot of thick black fluid into the palm of a boy's hand, and commanding him to see various people and things; of which practice Lane, in his Modern Egyptians, gives some curious disclosures.

Divining mirrors were not confined to the East. Dr. Dee was the first English impostor who vaunted the possession of one of these priceless treasures. He had for the *seer* one Keily, an Irishman; and to this, doubtless, was attributable the impression that prevailed among the astrologers and amateur spirit hunters, that when the spirits condescended to speak, they always gave speech with a very strong spice of the brogue. This "beryl," as it is called, was preserved among the Strawberry Hill curiosities, and fell under the hammer of George Robbins at the memorable sale. It proved to be a globe of *cannel coal*. In Aubrey's Miscellany there is an engraving of another larger crystal, and there are with it many wonderful stories. Yet, notwithstanding the magic capabilities of these mirrors, they went out of fashion until the beginning of the year 1850.

This revival and its consequences are like a page out of a silly romance. The story, if told by a disinterested historian, would require authentication as belonging to 1850. We therefore turn, by way of voucher, to a publication called Zadkiel's Almanac for 1851. At page 46, after referring to the existence of magic crystals at the present day, the writer, says, "One of large size was a few years ago brought over to England by a friend of Lady Blessington, after the sale of whose effects, it recently fell into the hands of a friend of mine; and, having tested its powers, I have resolved on giving my readers an account of this wonderful mode of communicating with the spirits of the dead. The crystal is spherical, and has been turned from a large mass of pure rock crystal. I have been shown some few others, but, with the exception of one shown me by Lord S., they are all much smaller. These smaller ones are said to be consecrated to angels of the planets, and are, therefore, far less powerful than Lady Blessington's crystal, which, being consecrated to the Archangel of the Sun, Michael, may be consulted during four hours each day, whereas the others can generally be used only for a very brief space of time; nor can very potent spirits be called into them, or made to render themselves visible. In this larger crystal is given most important information of the actual existence of the soul after death, and of the state in which it exists and will exist until the judgment."

"The first intimation we received," says Dickens, in his Household Words, "of the revival of this notable practice of divination, was about six months ago, when we were casually informed that the son of a distinguished officer of the royal navy was, at that time, frequently engaged in developing, before a few privileged friends, the extraordinary faculty of being able to hold intercourse with the world of spirits. It was added that the revelations made through the medium of this youth were of so wonderful a nature, and carried such conviction to the minds of those who listened, that they were declared to be the result of more than human power."

The conjurer was asked, on one occasion, to describe Lord Nelson. And, accordingly, the spirit, with an accuracy that was quite astonishing, considering that no portrait, bust, or statue of Nelson is known to exist, gave a full, true, and particular account of England's hero, describing him as a very thin man, in a cocked hat, with only one eye, one arm, &c.; and the truth of the description was declared to be something truly marvellous.

A demand was made that the spirit of a deceased brother of one of the querists should be summoned to appear. Presently he said, "I see him; he has curly hair, and stoops a good deal. I can't exactly see his features, but I think he squints." This account of her late brother's personal appearance, though not very flattering, satisfied the lady as far as it went; but being, like Macbeth,—

"... bent to know,

By the worst means, the worst,"

she required further proof of his identity. There was a pause for a minute or two, and then the spirit seer spoke again—"He has got a scroll in his hand, which he unfolds; there is this inscription on it, in *letters of fire*:—

'I AM TOM!'"

This sublime revelation was received with a degree of solemn awe, and with suppressed throes of well-bred laughter.

Other cases not a whit less marvellous have been described by the narrators, who could not be reasoned out of their absurdity, insisting that there could be no deception in the matter, on account of the means employed, and the evident sincerity of the *employés*! These means, they said, required that the person who looked into the crystal should be perfectly *pure*; that is to say, a child free from sin, and by no means given to lying, and that the form of adjuration used was, "*In nomine Domini*," &c.; Latin being, as is well known, the language which spirits of all denominations are most accustomed to. When interrogated after this fashion, the spirit, if evil, fled away howling; if good, it came, when called, unless particularly engaged *in the sun*; for it appears that it is to that planet almost all spirits go when their term of purgatory is over. It seems that the spirits would sometimes get out of breath, travelling so far, and talking so much; and they then had recourse to the expedient of *letters of fire*, which seemed to be *written* in various ways in the crystal; sometimes on flags, which the spirits hold up, but sometimes they are in *print*. In these letters of fire, the querist was counselled something like the following: "Be merry. Quarrel not. Keep your temper, and your children too. You are a good man, but try to be better. I am wanted. Let me go."

We subjoin the following as specimens of conversations heard by large parties of amazed, titled, and believing listeners: "Are you Pharaoh, that was king of Egypt?" "Yes." "Where do you dwell now?" "In Jupiter." "How long have you been there?" "About thirty years." "Where did you dwell till then?" "In the atmosphere, and was undergoing punishment till then."

"Were you king of Egypt when Moses was there?" "Yes, *and Aaron too.*" "Did you build the pyramids?" "*Some.*" "Were any built before your time?" "Yes." "Do you know how long the first was built before Christ?" "About three hundred years after Adam; it was built then." "Do you mean that it was built before the flood?" "No, it was not finished; the flood destroyed them." "What was the principal object of them?" "To hold the kings of Egypt." "Were there kings of Egypt so soon after the creation?" "Yes; that was the first country kings were in." "Were you drowned in the Red Sea?" "*Yes.*"

At one time Swedenborg volunteered to give information about Sir John Franklin, when the following dialogue took place: "What is the best way to communicate with him?" "By the natives; they speak to him sometimes." "Will he be home next summer?" "No." "Why?" "Because he cannot help himself; he is stopped by ice; but his heart does not fail him; he wants to explore." "How will he do for provisions?" "He will find *bears, dogs,* and *wolves.*" "Will he find the passage?" "No; there is a continent there." "But there is also a passage." "There is one, but he will not find it." "What latitude does he lie in chiefly?" "I do not know: *good by.*" It appears strange that Swedenborg, who knew so much, did not know this. But we learn in another place that "spirits do not *well* understand about latitude and longitude." Socrates's appearance is described as follows: "A tall, middle-aged man, rather bald, dressed with striped coarse trousers, very loose at the top, and tight at the bottom; a kind of frock, open in the front, and without sleeves. He is generally employed in singing praises, but was not quite happy." Alexander the Great appeared on horseback, in armor, the horse also in armor; deeply regrets killing Clitus, and all the murders he perpetrated; amuses himself in fighting his battles over again.

To give these things a sort of *éclat* and popularity with the public, Zadkiel sums up the whole in the following language: "In concluding this account, I may remark that *numerous children* have seen these visions, some of them the sons and daughters of persons of high rank; and that *several adults* have also seen visions, one of them a lady of title, and another a member of one of the highest families in England. It will be seen that delicacy prevents my naming individuals; but I can assure my readers that *above one hundred of the nobility,* and several hundreds of other highly respectable ladies and gentlemen, have examined this wonderful phenomenon, and have expressed the highest gratification and astonishment."

Dickens declares it to be "the fashion, especially among people of fashion, to point with pity to a tale of modern witchcraft, to an advertisement of a child's caul, or to the *bona fide* certificates of cases from the takers of quack medicines, and to deplore the ignorance of their inferiors. Delusions, however, of the grossest kind are not confined to the illiterate. A cloud of dupes have ever floated about in the higher regions of society; while it is quite a mistake to suppose that the refinements and discoveries of the nineteenth century have dispersed them. The reign of Queen Victoria, like that of Elizabeth and Anne, has its Dr. Dees, and Lillys, and Partridges, who are as successful as their precursors in gaining proselytes who can pay handsomely. Damsels of high degree, fresh from boarding school, with heads more full of sympathy for the heroes and heroines of fashionable novels, and ideas more fixed upon love affairs than on any legitimate studies, can easily find out, through mysteriously-worded advertisements in the Sunday papers, or through the ready agency of friends who have already become victims of the 'science' of astrology and magic, the whereabouts of these awful and wonderful beings. There are a number of styles and classes of them, all varying in appearance and mode of operations. There are the old women, who, consoled by the glories of their art, repine not at inhabiting comfortless garrets in the purlieus of the New Cut, Lambeth; and hiding their vocation under the mask of having stay laces or infallible corn plasters to sell, receive more visitors from the fashionable cream of Belgravia than from the dross of Bermondsey. Disguises are sometimes resorted to, and parties of titled ladies have been known to meet, and put on the habiliments of 'charwomen,' and to pass themselves off as dress-makers. There is an old man, with unshaven beard and seldom-washed face, who lives in more comfortable circumstances, with his son, in Southwark, (the favored district of the conjurers,) who, to keep up appearances, has 'Engineer' hugely engraved on a great brass plate over the door, who casts nativities, and foretells events of the future, for three or five shillings, as the appearance of the visitor will warrant him in demanding; receives all his votaries sitting at a terribly littered table of dirty paper, with a well-smoked clay pipe beside him. Passing to a higher grade, the 'agent,' or arranger of matters, legal, pecuniary, or domestic, only practises the black art for the love he bears it, and to oblige his friends, but never refuses a few shillings' fee, out of respect to the interests of the science. Nearly all his customers are people of title."

We now come to speak of events in our own country which seem to be somewhat akin to those which have so recently transpired in England. We allude to what are familiarly termed "rappers," or "knocking spirits," from the *noises* which they are said to make.

From a history of these *knockings*, as given in a pamphlet by Capron and Barron, of Auburn, New York, we learn that they were first heard in the family of Mr. Michael Weekman, in the town of Arcadia, Wayne county. He resided in the house where the noises were heard about eighteen months, and left it some time in the year 1847. He relates that one evening, about bedtime, he heard a rapping on the outside door, when he stepped to the door and opened it, but, to his surprise, found no one there. He went back, and proceeded to undress, when, just before getting into bed, he heard another rap at the door loud and distinct. He stepped to the door quickly and opened it, but, as before, found no one there. He stepped out, and looked around, supposing that some one was imposing upon him. He could discover no one, and went back into the house. After a short time he heard the rapping again; he stepped (it being often repeated) and held on the latch, so that he might ascertain if any one had taken that means to annoy him. The rapping was repeated; the door was instantly opened, but no one was to be seen. He could feel the jar of the door very plainly when the rapping was heard. As he opened the door, he sprung out, and went around the house, but no one was in sight. His family were fearful to have him go out, lest some one intended to harm him. It always remained a mystery to him; and finally, as the rapping did not at that time continue, it passed from his mind, till some time afterwards, when, one night, their little girl, then about eight years of age, was heard to scream from fright, so that the family were all alarmed by her cries, and went to her assistance. This was about midnight. She told them that something like a hand had passed over her face and head; that she had felt it on the bed and all over her, but did not feel alarmed until it touched her face.

It seems that Mr. Weekman soon after moved away from the house, and nothing more was heard of the rapping, or other manifestations, till it was occupied by the family of Mr. John D. Fox, who have since become so conspicuous with "the advent of spirits." In March, 1848, they, for the first time, heard the "mysterious sounds," which seemed to be like a slight knocking in one of the bed rooms on the floor. It was in the evening, just after they had retired. At that time the whole family occupied one room, and all distinctly heard the rapping. They arose, and searched with a light, but were unable to find the cause of the knocking. It continued that night until they all fell asleep, which was not until nearly or quite midnight. From this time the noise continued to be heard every night.

After having been disturbed and broken of their rest for several nights in a vain attempt to discover from whence the sounds proceeded, they resolved, on the evening of the 31st of March, that this night they would not be disturbed by it, whatever it might be. But Mr. Fox had not yet retired when the usual signs commenced. The girls, who occupied another bed in the same room, heard the sounds, and endeavored to imitate them by snapping their fingers. The attempt was made by the youngest girl, then about twelve years old. When she made the noise with her fingers, the sounds were repeated just as she made them. When she stopped snapping her fingers, the sounds stopped for a short time. One of the other girls then said, in *sport*, (for they were getting to be more amused than alarmed,) "Now do what I do; count one, two, three, four, five, six," &c., at the same time striking one hand in the other. The same number of blows or sounds were repeated as in the former case. Mrs. Fox then spoke, and said, "Count ten," and there were ten distinct strokes or sounds. She then said, "Will you tell the age of Cathy?" (one her children;) and it was given by the same number of raps that she was years of age. In like manner the age of her different children was told correctly by this *unseen visitor.*

Mrs. Fox then asked, if it was a *human* being that made the noise, to manifest it by making the same noise. There was no answer to this request. She then asked if it was a *spirit,* and if so to manifest it by making two distinct sounds. Instantly she heard two raps, as she desired. She then proceeded to know or inquire if it was an injured spirit, and if so to answer in the same way, and the rapping was repeated. In this way it answered her until she ascertained that it purported to be the spirit of a man who was murdered in that house by a person that had occupied it some years before; that he was a *pedler,* and that he was murdered for his money. To the question *how old he was,* there were *thirty-one* distinct raps. By the same means it was ascertained that he was a married man, and had left a wife and five children; that his wife had been dead two years.

We might relate a little different manœuvre in the case of the *ghost* that appeared in Waltham, Massachusetts, a few years since. A superstitious old man, by the name of McClarren, a mechanic, purchased a lot of turf that had been piled up in a meadow about half way between his workshop and place of residence. Upon returning to his work from supper, he used to take a basket with him, and fill it at the turf heap on his return late in the evening. It was on one of these occasions that the reputed ghost first appeared to him, and caused him some alarm, when he dare not linger to reconnoitre this strange and unexpected visitor. He resolved, however, to muster courage the next evening to accost the figure, should it again appear to him. Accordingly, he went with a large Bible open in his hands; and as the ghost appeared, he followed it till it crossed a ditch, when he was requested by the same to proceed no farther. Thus they stood, facing each other, on either side of the ditch, when the following conversation took place between them:—

Ques. By McClarren. "I demand of you, in the name of Jesus Christ, our once crucified God, whether you are mortal or immortal?"

Ans. "I am not mortal."

Ques. "What, then, are you?"

Ans. "I am the spirit of a murdered man."

Ques. "By whom were you murdered?"

Ans. "By ——, of Waltham."

Ques. "Where does your body lie?"

Ans. "In yonder pond, behind me."

It is supposed that this affair was got up in an innocent mood, merely to test the strength of McClarren's faith in ghosts. But it caused a wide-spread excitement; and some, who were thought to be concerned in its projection, were prosecuted and brought before a justice for examination, although nothing was proved. McClarren testified under oath, that he believed it to be a real ghost; "*its tones*," he said, "were so *unearthly*," "and when it moved its motion was not like that in walking, but it glided along like a swan, or a boat in the water." He was neither to be reasoned nor laughed out of it. He would believe it to the day of his death. You might as well tell him he was not a living being, as to tell him he had not seen a living ghost.

The advocates of the "influx from the world of spirits into our own" claim in its behalf many astonishing miracles. Chairs, tables, and beds are moved up or down, to and fro, &c. At Auburn, New York, on one occasion, sounds on the wall, bureau, table, floor, and other places were heard as loud as the striking with a hammer. The table was moved about the room, and turned over and back. Two men in the company undertook to hold a chair down, while, at their request, a spirit moved it; and, notwithstanding they exerted all their strength, the chair could not be held still by them—a proof that spirits are far more strong and powerful than men. On another occasion, the sounds proper to a carpenter's shop were heard, apparently proceeding from the wall and table. Sawing, planing, and pounding with a mallet were imitated, it is said, *to the life.* Some gentlemen were at the house of the Fox family at one time, and were conducted into a *dark room.* They called for the sounds to be made like a band of martial music. As they requested, the sounds were produced; the playing of the instruments and the heavy beating of the bass drum were perfectly imitated, together with the sound of the roar of distant cannon. Shall we not gather from this, that in the spirit world they have their bands of music and companies of artillery, the same as in this world? We are also told of the spirit or spirits playing on a guitar in a *dark* room, the guitar being taken from the hands of those who held it and put in tune, and played while it passed around the room above their heads. On one occasion, as it is said, it played an accompaniment, for nearly two hours, to some persons engaged in singing, being very exact both in time and tune. On one occasion, while several ladies were present, some of them requested that the spirits would take their hair down. Accordingly it was done. One of them had her hair taken down and done up in a twist, and one of them had hers braided in four strands. Sometimes persons have felt a hand passing over or touching their arms, head, or face, leaving a feeling of electricity upon the part touched; and the hand that thus touches them will, by request, instantly change from a natural warmth to the coldness of ice.

In answer to the question, "Why do these spirits require a dark room to play upon instruments of music, or to take hold of persons," they answer by saying that "they assume a tangible form in order to do these things, and we are not yet prepared for such a visitation."

To the inquiry how it is they make the rapping noises that generally accompany their visits to this world, they answer, that "they are made by the will of the spirits causing a concussion of the atmosphere, and making the sounds appear in whatever place they please."

A Mrs. Draper, of Rochester, New York, had an interview with Dr. Franklin, at one time, while she was in a magnetized state. She said he appeared to be busily employed in establishing a line of communication between the two worlds by means of these "rappings." On another occasion, while in a clairvoyant state, at her own house, sounds were heard in exact imitation of those heard in the telegraph office. These sounds were so unusual, that Miss Margaretta Fox, who was present, became alarmed, and said, "What does all this mean?" Mrs. Draper replied, "*He is trying the batteries.*" Soon there was a signal for the alphabet, and the following communication was spelled out to the company present. "Now I am ready, my friends. There will be great changes in the nineteenth century. Things that now look dark and mysterious to you, will be laid plain before your sight. Mysteries are going to be revealed. The world will be enlightened. I sign my name, Benjamin Franklin."

It seems that, in the early history of these rappings, they used to be without any limitations as to whether persons were in a magnetized state or not. The first we learn of magnetism being employed as a *medium* of communication is in the case of a daughter of Lyman Granger, in Rochester, New York. For a long time, answers could be obtained by any *two* (why *two*?) of the family standing near each other. And in the freedom of the answers, no preference seemed to be manifested towards any particular members of the family. At length, one of his daughters was placed under the influence of magnetism, and became clairvoyant. From that time none of the family could get communications unless the daughter who was magnetized was present. Why the communications should leave all the family except the magnetized daughter, after they once had free conversation without her, remains to be explained. The whole business now seems to be pretty much, if not wholly, monopolized by the clairvoyants. They seem to be employed as agents, or mediums of correspondence, between the two worlds, acting as interpreters between two classes of beings, or beings existing in two different states, *natural* and *spiritual*. They act as a kind of *spiritual postmasters* between the two countries. We find *spiritual letter paper*, and *envelopes* to enclose the same, advertised for those who wish to avail themselves of an opportunity to write to their deceased friends in the other spheres. Letters said to have been written in the spirit world have been transmitted through the established mediums to friends in this world, and have been published in some of the papers devoted to these subjects. In the New York Daily Tribune of February 28, 1851, we find the prospectus of a quarto journal, to be published in Auburn, "to be dictated by spirits out of the flesh, and by them edited, superintended, and controlled. Its object is the disclosure of truth from Heaven, guiding mankind into open vision of paradise, and open communication with redeemed spirits. The circle of apostles and prophets are its conductors from the interior, holding control over its columns, and permitting no article to find place therein unless originated, dictated, or admitted by them: they acting under direction of the Lord Supreme."

We hope the information coming through its columns will be more reliable than the communications from some of the "rapping spirits." No dependence whatever can be placed upon them. They are so blundering, awkward, and uncertain, and even trickish and deceitful, that they spoil all our notions of the dignify and purity—the *spirituality*, in fact—of the spiritual world. The advocates of the manifestations attribute the fault to *ignorant spirits*, who do not know whether the matter they attempt to speak of be true or not. Swedenborg says, "There are some spirits so ignorant that they do not know but they are the ones called for, when another is meant. And the only way to detect them, in speaking, is by the difference of sound—that made by intelligent spirits being clear and lively, and that of the ignorant being low and muffled, like the striking of the hand upon a carpet."

It is contended by the authors of the pamphlet from which we quote, that these ignorant spirits will ultimately *progress* to a state of *intelligence*. But this idea of *progression* seems to be at variance with the observations of a writer in the Boston Post, who was astonished at the wonderful precocity of little infants in the spirit world. "I have known," says he, "the spirit of a child, only eighteen months old when he died, and only three months in the second sphere, show as much *intelligence*, and as perfect a command of our language, as Dr. Channing himself seems to possess." On the other hand, when I find that "the spirit of Dr. Channing cannot express an idea above the rudimental conception of a mere child, I am forced to the conclusion that his mental endowments must have greatly deteriorated since he left us."

It is said that the theological teachings of these spirits generally agree with those of Davis, Swedenborg, and others who have claimed to receive their impressions from spirits. Accordingly, we find them using the term *higher and lower spheres*, instead of *heaven and hell*. Swedenborg prophesied that the year 1852 would be the one to decide the fate of his church or his doctrines; and Capron and Barron tell us that "the probabilities now seem to be that his general spiritual theory will, not far from that time, be very generally received." We presume that the "mysterious rappings" are considered by them as so many omens of such an event. And we may reasonably conclude that they are as *decisive* tests, as *sure* prognostications, as were the various celestial signs of the coming of the end of the world in 1843. The believers in the "harmonial philosophy" have their miracles in attestation of their theory; and so of the Millerites. On Saturday evening, January 18, 1851, we are told by La Roy Sunderland, that Mrs. Cooper (clairvoyant medium) was taken to Cambridge, by Mr. Fernald and a friend, for the purpose of visiting a gentleman who had been confined by a spinal difficulty some ten years or more. The spirits gave beautiful responses for his consolation, and in the sight of all present, *the sick man and his bed* were moved by spiritual hands alone. The sick man and the "bed whereon he lay" were both moved by attending angels, without any human power. And more recently, a Mr. Gordon, it is said, has been taken up and his body moved some distance entirely by spiritual hands. Were such miracles ever wrought in favor of Millerism? Most assuredly, if we are to believe the Millerites themselves; and even more in favor of witchcraft also. At a meeting of the friends of Millerism, held in Waltham, in 1842, a lady was taken from her seat by some unseen power, and carried up to the ceiling of the room; and she afterwards declared that it was done without any effort on her part. More recently, (1851,) another lady of the same place testifies that she has, in a similar manner, been taken from her seat in church and carried up above the tops of the pews. And at times, at the advent meetings, strange noises have been heard, houses also have been shaken, mirrors shattered to pieces, and furniture broken, and all have been considered by the Adventists as so many auguries or signs of the approaching dissolution of all things, to take place in 1843.

We have already made mention of the fact, in another place, that bewitched persons used to be carried through the air, on brooms and spits, to distant meetings, or Sabbaths, of witches. But we will now give a case to the point.

On the 8th of September, 1692, Mary Osgood, wife of Captain Osgood, of Andover, was taken before John Hawthorne, and other of their majesties' justices, when she confessed that, about two years before, she was carried through the air, in company with Deacon Fry's wife, Ebenezer Baker's wife, and Goody Tyler, to Five Mile Pond, where she was baptized by the devil, and that she was transported back again through the air, in company with the forenamed persons, in the same manner as she went, and *believes* they were carried on a *pole*! She was asked by one of the justices, how many persons were upon the pole; to which she answered, As I said before, viz., four persons, and no more, but whom she had named above.

Are not these cases to be relied upon as much as those related by Mr. Sunderland? Could not *four* respectable ladies tell whether they were *actually* carried through the air on a pole or *not*? *Could* they be deceived? Possibly, in the days of chloroform, or ether, it might have been the case; but not at the period in which it actually occurred.

Some of the bewitched persons, as in the case of Elizabeth Knap, of Groton, alarmed the people by their *ventriloqual* powers, in imitating sounds and languages. And it would be nothing strange if some of our modern witches were in possession of the same talent. No wonder that the editor of one of the Boston papers should have ventured the opinion, that if some of these persons had lived two hundred years ago, they would have been hanged for witchcraft.

It appears to us, that if we believe in all that is alleged of the rapping spirits, and their manifestations, we must be prepared to indorse all that has been published of witches and ghosts, spooks and hobgoblins, in every age of the world, which, at present, we are not at all inclined to do. We do not believe that any of the noises heard, or any of the information given, has proceeded from beings out of the normal state. We are rather inclined to adhere to the sentiment contained in the old couplet:—

"Where men *believe* in witches, witches are;

But where they don't believe, there are none there."

We once went to stay over night in a house said to be haunted, the house being empty at the time, the family who had occupied it having actually been frightened away by the noises they had heard. But, strange to tell, we did not hear any *noises*, neither did we expect to. There was a house in Green Street, Boston, formerly occupied by the celebrated Dr. Conway, which, after his decease, was said to be haunted. A young man of our acquaintance never passed that house late at night but every window in it appeared to be illuminated. And finally, he became so alarmed about it, that as soon as he approached the vicinity of the house, he would commence running, and continue to run till it was out of sight. We have frequently known him to cross the ice on Charles River to avoid passing the house. And still, we often passed the same house, at late hours of the night, without seeing any thing unusual. And we know of no reason why, unless it was because we did not believe in such things, which our friend actually did. *Faith* alone made the difference.

One of the believers in the "spirit rappings" tells us that "*if* these things are emanations from the spirit world, we are bound to believe them." True, *if* they are; but this little conjunctive *if* is a word of very *doubtful* meaning. We have already shown how Mr. Miller kept the whole world standing thirty years on this same little *if*; and then it did not end in 1843, as he supposed it would. We must, therefore, be cautious how we depend upon a simple *if*.

But we are told that, as honest persons, we are bound to believe what we cannot disprove by actual demonstration. But let us examine this for a moment. The Greenlanders have an idea that thunder is caused by two old women flapping seal skins in the moon. Now, who has ever been up in the moon to ascertain whether it is so or not? Again, they say that the Aurora Borealis is owing to the spirits of their fathers frisking at football. Who can say it is not so? And yet *we* reject such belief on account of its apparent absurdity. Some of the ancients have told us that the earth stands upon the back of a tortoise, or upon that of an elephant; and yet, without investigation, a majority of mankind reject the idea as being perfectly ridiculous. We might here remark, that no less a scholar than the great mathematician Kepler attempted to prove that the earth is a vast animal, and that the tides are occasioned by the heavings of its prodigious lungs.

Many of the performances of jugglers and ventriloquists puzzle us, and yet we do not believe there is any thing supernatural in them. Signor Blitz once called upon the ladies in the hall where he was giving an exhibition to pass him a handkerchief with their name stamped upon it, and he would put it into a pistol and fire it off in their presence, and it should be found in the steeple of a church some quarter of a mile distant, and yet not a window or a door should be open on the occasion. A committee of honest and respectable men were despatched from the hall to the house of the church sexton, the keys procured, with a lantern, when the belfry was ascended, the handkerchief found hanging on the tongue of the bell, and returned to the lady, who instantly recognized it as the identical handkerchief she passed into the hands of the performer. Now, who could prove that the thing alleged was not *actually* done? and yet who will *believe* that it was?

We have heard distant sounds of music, and other imitations of men, birds, and animals, that deceived our sense of hearing, knowing that they were produced by the power of ventriloquism. We have seen things moved from place to place by *magnetic attraction*, and we do not think it at all strange that so light an instrument as a guitar could be thus attracted to different parts of a room by an *unseen power*, especially in a *dark* room, and its tones be imitated by a being as yet in the *normal* state. A guitar will give vibrations of its tones to the concussions of the air, caused by the conversation of persons present; and a stranger to the fact might possibly interpret these vibrations as something quite mysterious, and suppose the instrument, as it stood alone, to be touched by some spirit hand. When people's minds, or their imaginations, get wrought up to a certain pitch, the most trifling things are looked upon as wonderful phenomena. Every thing is *new*, and *strange*, and *appalling*. We hear of the doings of the spirits at Rochester, and other places, and which are called the "ushering in of a *new science*." "We know of what we speak," says the pamphlet before us, "we *know* they are *facts, strange, new*, and to many *wonderful*." (See page 43.) And yet the authors introduce several pages from a work by Dr. Adam Clarke to show that, as early as 1716, the Wesley family were troubled by noises made by the "knocking spirits," and that "the present manifestations have no claim to the credit of originality." The cracking of hazel nuts upon Martin Luther's bed posts, and the racket and rumbling upon his chamber stairs, as if many empty barrels and hogs-heads had been tumbling down, claim still greater antiquity, and belong to the same category or chapter of wonderful events.

It is said to be impossible that any mere human being could inform persons, with whom they never had any previous knowledge or acquaintance, of the past, present, and future events of their lives—whether they are married or single, the number of their children living and dead, age, health, business, letters expected, the whereabout of long-absent friends, &c. It is supposed that such information must indeed emanate from the spirit world. Yet precisely such things are and always have been told, more or less, by astrologers and fortune tellers, without any pretensions to being in league with spirits of the other worlds. We have said that fortune tellers do not always tell correctly; but, as poor an opinion as we have of them, we will venture to assert that they are full as correct, if not more so, in the information they give, as the members of the Fox family, or any of their contemporaries, of the alleged *spiritual* manifestations.

Persons of sane mind, though ever so ignorant of arithmetic or orthography, can tell at least how many children they have, and are usually able to spell their own names; but one who has spent a good deal of time in witnessing the performances of the *spirit rappers*, says, "They seem to be unwilling or unable to answer purely test questions, like that of answering their own names. I have never known them to do this," says he, "though often solicited." He also speaks of their great deficiency in mathematics, not being able to enumerate the number of children they have on earth with any thing like accuracy. "I am aware that such questions have sometimes been correctly answered, and I have heard them so answered; but I have much more frequently known them to refuse entirely, or to do it very awkwardly, or to fail entirely in the attempt. Out of five numbers four were erroneously selected as the right one. The fifth was right, of course. This goes to show, at least, that spirits have greatly *deteriorated*, rather than *improved*, while inhabiting the celestial spheres." But this is not all. The facility of communication between the two classes of beings is also on the decline. The time was when ghosts or spirits held free conversation with those they visited, without calling in the aid of clairvoyancy or electricity. Neither did they resort, like modern spirits, to the slow and clumsy mode of communication, through the letters of the alphabet. In spelling out a sentence by letters, one of the ladies commences repeating the alphabet; and when the desired letter is mentioned, a rap is heard. In this slow and tedious process, long sentences are communicated. No wonder that the slowness of the mode of communication should be considered as "perfectly appalling." And then, too, the substance of these communications is too absurd and ridiculous to be believed. We might here refer to the information given by the prophet Swedenborg himself, in relation to the condition of the pious Melancthon in the future state, that he was sometimes in an excavated stone chamber, and at other times in hell; and when in the chamber, he was covered with bear skins to protect him from the cold; and that he refuses to see visitors from this world on account of the filthiness of his apartment. This is about as probable and interesting as the account given by a female clairvoyant in Cleveland, Ohio, who says that she has (just) had an interview with Tom Paine, "who recants his errors, and is at present stopping with General Washington and Ethan Allen, at a hotel kept by John Bunyan."

We here introduce the following from one of the Boston papers:—

"*The 'Spiritual Rappings' exploded.*—There is a good article under this head, on the first page, to which we invite attention. The writer is an accomplished scholar, an able physician, and one of the first and best magnetizers in this country. He has investigated the 'rappings'—tested them theoretically and practically, and 'exploded' them, if our readers have not already done so for themselves. His communication is entitled to weight, and if circulated, as it should be, among the credulous and unsuspecting, might save some from the pitiful effects of a mischievous, absurd, and contemptible superstitious delusion."

The article is as follows:—

"About the 16th of December last, I called on Mr. Sunderland, in good faith, in order to hear and see manifestations from the spirit world. He received me in a friendly manner, and, with a young lady who was with me, seated me in the spirit room. We had to wait an hour or more, and while seated we devoutly invoked the spirits. Finding them silent, I put on them some of my most powerful mesmeric electric formula. They persevered, however, in preserving profound silence.

"When, however, the medium, Mrs. Cooper, had arrived, and seven of us, four gentlemen and three ladies, were seated round a square centre table, the responses were made, and came freely. The young lady with me, willing to believe, but wishing to know with absolute certainty, before she assented to the truth of the proposition, that the rappings were made by spirits, and not by the persons engaged in the business, had seated herself about three feet from the table, so that she could see under it. The following dialogue then ensued between Mrs. Cooper, her adopted sister, and the young lady:—

"'Will you sit close to the table, miss?'

"'If they are spirits, they can rap just as well where I am. I am willing to be convinced, and where I am I can hear perfectly well.'

"'The rule is, to sit close to the table.'

"'I will not disturb, but choose to sit where I am.'

"'If you will not comply with the regulation, you had better go into the other room.'

"'I came to know, and I shall sit where I am.'

"She was inflexible, and the work proceeded. When my turn came, I could put no test question, and was so told. I saw and felt that there was collusion, and, ashamed of myself as being the dupe of supposed and known imposition, after enduring the hour's sitting, I arose with the full conviction that all was the effect of bones and muscles, and of mesmeric action and reaction on the subjects themselves. While we were examining a piano which was used on such occasions, and our backs were turned towards the table, standing partly sidewise, I caught a glimpse of Mrs. Cooper's foot in the very position and act of commencing a spirit somerset on the table. She looked confused. I appeared not to have fully recognized any thing wrong, thanked them for their father's kindness and their attention, and left the domicil of the 'spiritual philosopher' under a full, stern, and abiding conviction that *there* was not the abiding place of invisible beings—that all was mechanical which we heard, and all that any one had heard or seen was mechanical or mesmeric.

"The second opportunity I had of testing the truth or falsity of these spirit communications was in the city of Lowell. Every thing was favorable as to place, time, and company. My eyes were every where, and raps came seldom and solitary. The medium dropped from between his fingers a small black pencil, about two inches long, with which I believe he made the raps.

After it fell, we heard no more. He looked despairingly disappointed, soon went into a trance, arose, locked us into the room, and when the hour had transpired, came out voluntarily.

"Invited by a friend who was anxious to convince me more fully, and especially to convert the young lady who was with me at Mr. Sunderland's, he called at my house with the medium, and was received into my office. The young lady requested that we should stand around the table, and no one touch it. We did so. On the first response, she exclaimed, indignantly, addressing the medium, 'That, sir, was from your foot; I heard it distinctly!' He looked guilty, and his eyes flashed with anger. He asked the spirits if it was not 'nonsense,' and received the response from the foot, 'yes,' and left, evidently highly incensed.

"I determined to give one more trial to the spirits. In this latter case, there were the three raps, clear and strong, and the answers highly satisfactory, as far as they went. But the difficulty was, that the spirits were capricious, and would respond only to just such as they saw fit; and the medium was pretty well acquainted with me. The perfect regularity of the knocks, and the sound, convinced me that, in this instance, it was purely mechanical. I endeavored to get the secret from the medium, and the answer was, 'If I should tell you, you would be as wise as myself.' She evidently knew how it was done.

"I will now state a few facts, and conclude. 1. Wood is an excellent conductor of sounds. A small worm, called at the south a sawyer, and sought for angling, can be heard three yards, as it gnaws between the wood and bark of a fallen pine; and the slightest scratch of a pin, on the end of an isolated mast, sixty feet long, can be heard distinctly.

"2. In mesmeric operations, we well know that individuals *can be made to hear and see things that never occurred or existed*, and yet the subjects remain unconscious that they have been made the *subjects of mesmeric hallucination!*

"3. Persons highly observant and susceptible can, by their eye and feeling, when they put themselves into a semi-abnormal condition, tell, in many instances nine times out of ten, who is and who is not a believer, *and what is in the mind of the inquirer.*

"4. Mediums are invariably of this character.

"5. In matters of faith, friendship, love, or the spirit world, many are willing to be deceived; and when they fall into the hands of the shrewd and designing, who can appear the impersonation of truth, virtue, honesty, and even piety itself, they are emphatically *humbugged*, and give their money and their testimony to confirm the fraud.

"Lastly. Many are so sincere and honest in their intentions, that it is not in their hearts to believe that some of our most respectable men, even clergymen, would lend their names to sustain any thing but what they had believed and tested as a reality, and therefore themselves believe.

"Now, Mr. Editor, from all that I have seen and know of these spiritual communications, as 'rappings,' and from all these facts, I am free to declare, that I believe them an arrant humbug, and one, too, of the most pernicious tendency. They can all be traced to a human agency, as either mechanical or mesmeric, alone or combined; and I will give my right hand to any medium whose operation and device I cannot fully discover, trace, and demonstrate, as deducible from either the one or both of these sources, *and from no other.*"

A correspondent of the Boston Traveller, in a communication dated New York, January 22, 1852, says, "I look upon the delusion as I do upon a contagious disease. It is a moral epidemic. Any man of peculiar diathesis may be its victim. It spreads by sympathy and by moral infection. Men of standing and intellect gravely and seriously affirm that they have seen a man rise and float about the room like a feather, till some unbelieving wretch approaches and breaks the spell, when the aerial swimmer falls suddenly to the floor. Franklin, Washington, and all the signers of the Declaration of Independence, have visited them, and these departed worthies sanction any doctrine which the uninitiated may happen to entertain before consulting them." A. J. Davis says, "There is a class of spirits who dwell in divine love more than in divine wisdom, and who are easily influenced to *feel* precisely what the majority of those who consult them *feel* and think, and under peculiar circumstances will say *precisely* what the questioning minds of the circle may *ardently* and *positively* desire. Affectionate spirits—those dwelling in the *love circles*—are readily influenced to approve the desires of the hearts of those with whom they commune on earth; as in our homes, the infant, by virtue of its cries and positive entreaties, captivates the affectionate, and perhaps intelligent, mother, who, consequently, forthwith coincides with her child's desires, submitting her judgment to its powerful appeals. Thus it is, through the power of sympathy, spirits of the other world gratify all our thoughts and desires." This is the *opinion* of Mr. Davis, which may pass for what it is worth. We never indorse his spiritual notions.

To give an idea of the conduct exhibited at the circles, or meetings, of the "harmonials," we submit the following from the Springfield Republican of January, 1852:—

"When we entered the hall, the meeting had not commenced, and all parties were engaged in a lively chat. Soon there was a spontaneous coming to order, and the ladies formed a circle around a table. The gentlemen then formed a larger circle, entirely surrounding the ladies. A good hymn was given out and sung. During the singing, we noticed one lady growing excessively pale and cadaverous. Then her hands began to twitch, and she commenced pounding upon the table. Directly opposite her, a young woman was undergoing the process of being magnetized by the spirits, while she, as we were informed, was resisting them. Her hands were drawn under the table by sudden and powerful jerks, and every muscle in her body seemed to be agitated with the most powerful commotion, as if she were acted upon in every part by shocks of electricity. This continued for ten or fifteen minutes, until she was, at last, in a state apparently resembling the magnetic sleep.

"Another lady, with a fine eye and an intellectual cast of countenance, was then moved to write, which she did, while her eyes stared and rolled as if in a state of frenzy, and every muscle seemed strained to its utmost tension. She wrote absolutely furiously, but no one but the spirits could read it, and it was passed over to another medium, who announced it a message of such utter unimportance that we have forgotten it. A brawny blacksmith was among the mediums, but he did nothing but pound on the table, and write the word 'sing.' The famous medium Gordon was there, too, and he went through various contortions—got down upon his knees, stood upon his seat, and stretched up his arms and fingers, trembling all the while, as if in the highest state of nervous excitement. Once he was twitched bodily under the table, uttering a scream as he went. At times, the different mediums would rise, spread their arms, slap the table, and throw their hands into motions almost inconceivably rapid.

"One of the mediums, a young woman, arose by the dictation and powerful urging of the spirits, and delivered a rambling sermon. It abounded in quotations from the Bible and the doctrines of Universalism.

"But it was when the singing was in progress that the spirits and the mediums were in the highest ecstasy. Then the latter would pound, and throw their arms around, and point upwards, in the most fantastic manner possible. And thus, with singing, and pounding, and reading the Bible, and writing, and preaching, the evening passed away; and while Old Hundred was being sung, the spirits gave their good night to the circle.

"We can give but a faint idea of this scene. It is one we shall never forget, and we only wish that the respectable men we saw there, the men of age and experience, the young men and young women, could understand the pity with which a man without the circle of their sympathy regarded them. With the light of reason within them, with minds not untaught by education, and with the full and perfect revelation of God's will in their very hands, it was indeed most pitiable to see them swallowing these fantastic mummeries, and mingling them, in all their wild, furious, and unmeaning features, with the worship of Him who manifests himself in the 'still small voice.'

"Of the sincerity of the majority of those present we have no doubt; but that there are rank impostors in this town, who are leading astray the credulous, we have as little doubt. The most that we saw on Saturday night was mesmerism, and the rest a very transparent attempt at deception. At any rate, if it was any thing else, we should attribute it to any thing but good spirits. Were we a devil, and should we wish to see how foolish we could make people appear, we should choose this way. O men and women, do have done with such outrageous nonsense."

Some have been most grossly deceived, and even made insane, by being made to believe that they were magnetized by spirits. This was the case with one of the celebrated Hutchinson singers—Judson J. Hutchinson. Mr. Sunderland, in the fourth number of the Spiritual Philosopher, observes as follows: "We shall hear of communications from 'prophets,' 'apostles,' 'kings,' and 'statesmen,' and of divers 'revelations,' said to be made by them. We shall hear of human beings said to be magnetized by spirits. But the *good* and the *true* will know and understand how easy it is for some to become 'magnetized' by their own *ideas*, and to take for 'revelations' *the fancies of their own brains.* The notion about mortals being magnetized by spirits is a mistake, an *error*; and it was this error which was the principal cause of all the real difficulty in the case of Judson J. Hutchinson. Mr. H. was made to believe that he was in company with his deceased brother, and that his own deceased children came and sat upon his knees, and put their arms about his neck. When he found himself sinking into an *abnormal state*, he was told to believe that it was *the spirits*, and that there was nothing *human* about it. This, of course, Mr. H. was ready to believe. He had heard of others being magnetized by spirits, and they were happy, very happy. And as this seemed to promise him *approximation* to the spirit world, for which he was earnestly longing, he readily gave himself entirely to that idea." The operator, Mr. Hazard, of Rochester, New York, suggested that Mr. Hutchinson should ask the spirits to move his (Mr. H.'s) hand to the top of his own head, that then he (Mr. H.) might know it was they. "But the operator should have known," says Mr. Sunderland, "that his *suggesting* it to the mind of Mr. Hutchinson, in the manner he did, or, if Mr. Hutchinson's own mind was *directed* to the movement of his own hand, *that* was sufficient to cause his hand to move, *even if there had been no spirits in existence.* And so, when Mr. H. went to Cleveland, the difficulty was increased by a repetition of the cause. He fell into the same state again, of course, when similar *associations* brought it up before his mind; and there he was again told by a clairvoyant lady, that she 'saw the spirits' (his brother Benjamin and Swedenborg) operating upon him. The effect was, to render him *insane*."

His brother Jesse says, that "the shock was too great for Judson, on account of his bodily weakness, and that his feeble nature was too fine strung to bear up against the severe attacks, and it was with great difficulty he was brought back to Milford, New Hampshire." While in this state, Mr. Sunderland was sent for, and staid with him three days and three nights, to render him assistance. Mr. S. says, "He was unfortunate in being told that he was magnetized by spirits, and still more so, perhaps, in the treatment he met with from some *uncongenial spirits* in Syracuse and in Worcester." From this, as well as from some other unfortunate cases, persons are admonished to be careful to refrain from visiting such impostors.

Some have been told that St. Paul, St. Peter, St. Luke, and Timothy, were present, and answered questions put to them; but Mr. Davis and Mr. Sunderland declare it to be false. Mr. Davis says, "This point I have been led to investigate carefully; and at no one of the *circles* referred to do I discover, upon the most critical interior retrospection, a *single* communication from the veritable St. Paul, nor from any one of his glorious compeers."

So of Benjamin Franklin, who, it is said, has never condescended to converse but a very few times with earthly beings, though his name is often quoted in connection with clairvoyancy. The reason he is said to assign to Mr. Davis is, that he cannot "prevent the almost exact human imitations of his vibrations; and that they produce so much confusion and contradiction, that, he thinks it best to wait until some further improvement can be made in the mode of communication between the two worlds." Yet how many are told that they have been put in communication with Franklin!

Mr. Sunderland says, "We need the same conditions, or guaranties, for believing *spirits*, that we do for believing *human* testimony." Speaking of those clairvoyants who are supposed to be exalted into the spirit sphere, so as to see and converse with spirits, he says, "Whether they do, really, see the spirits, whom they think they do, must be determined by other things besides their own testimony. We are not obliged to take their own mere *ipse dixit* upon this, any more than upon any other subject." And as yet, as has been remarked by Dr. Phelps, *there is no proof that what purports to be a revelation from spirits is the work of spirits at all.* Mr. Sunderland, for all we can see, is liable to be in an error, as well as others; and all the evidence he gives us that he has had interviews and holds conversations with spirits is that of his own testimony alone. And so of Mr. Davis.

We have said that no dependence whatever can be placed upon the rapping spirits. Dr. Phelps, of Stratford, Connecticut, once heard a very loud rapping under the table while at his breakfast. "I asked if it was my sister. The answer was, 'Yes.' 'Well,' said I, 'if you are the spirit of my sister, you can tell me how many children you have in this world.' So the spirit commenced counting, and counted up to twenty-five, when I pronounced it a *lying* spirit. I asked it, 'Are you unhappy?' It answered, 'Yes.' 'Can I do you any good?' 'Yes.' 'How?' The spirit then called for the alphabet, and spelled out, 'Give me a glass of fresh gin.' 'What will you do with it,' said I. *'Put it to my mouth.'* I asked, 'Where is your mouth?' No answer."

Letters, and lines written upon scraps of paper, have, it is said, been sent from the other world. The following was dropped from the ceiling of Mrs. Phelps's parlor when she and others were present.

"Sir,—Sir Sambo's compliments, and begs the ladies to accept as a token of his esteem." Other papers have been similarly written upon, and signed "Sam Slick," "The Devil," "Beelzebub," "Lorenzo Dow," &c.

On the 15th of March, 1850, a large turnip was thrown against Dr. Phelps's parlor window, having several characters carved out upon it, somewhat resembling the Chinese characters. A *fac-simile* of them may be found in Davis's explanation of Modern Mysteries, page 55.

Some may receive such things as emanations from the spirit world; but to us they seem too simple and puerile to be considered as having any thing to do with the higher spheres.

Dr. Phelps, who has been witness to every species of manœuvre of the alleged spirit rappers, says that he has become fully satisfied that no reliance whatever is to be placed on their communications, either as a source of valuable information, or as a means of acquiring truth. "I am satisfied," says he, "that their communications are *wholly worthless*. They are often contradictory, often prove false, frequently trifling and nonsensical, and more in character with what might be expected of a company of loafers on a spree than from spirits returned from a world of retribution to 'tell the secrets of their prison house.'"

With regard to moving tables, chairs, beds, &c., Mr. Davis says that, "at a circle of friends in Bridgeport, Connecticut, there was a large congregation of spirits, who, from a distance of eighty miles, or thirty above the atmosphere of our earth, directed a mighty column of vital electricity and magnetism, which column or current, penetrating all intermediate substances, and by a process of infiltration, entered the fine particles of matter which composed the table, and raised it, several successive times, three or four feet from the floor!" This we are to receive upon his authority, or upon the testimony of those who may say they saw the table moved. But if the operator can *make things appear* that *never occurred or existed,* and can *imagine* a thing, and have that *imagination transferred to others,* then what evidence have we that *spirits* are concerned in the transaction? Just none at all. A while ago, we heard of an Italian, at the Massachusetts Hospital, who could raise tables from the floor without touching them; and the art of so doing, he said, he learned in Italy. And how are we to account for the Millerites and others being so raised, as they believed? Are they not as much to be credited as those who profess a belief in the miracles of the "harmonial philosophers"? For ourselves, we are satisfied that such things, for the most part, are but a delusion, whether they are alleged to take place among those supposed to be bewitched, the Adventists, or the harmonials.

As to the *rapping noises*, we are inclined to think they may have something to do with the knee and toe joints, and that the two performers usually sit together, in order the better to alternate with, and *spell* or relieve each other. Upon a fair trial, it certainly has been proved that the noises cannot be produced when the joints are grasped firmly by another. But it may be doubted by some whether the joints can be made to produce the distinct rappings that are sometimes heard. We think they can. A few years ago, a boy in London gave exhibitions of what was termed "*chin music.*" It was done by striking the fists upon the lower jaw. By this practice he was able to produce quite loud and distinct sounds, and play a variety of tunes, to the amusement of the public. The sounds were made by the finger joints, it was supposed; and perhaps the jaw bone may have contributed its share in the performance. The sounds given by the "rapping spirits" are by no means so remarkable as many suppose. They are often quite indistinct, and nearly inaudible. Unless a person was possessed of a large share of credulity, he would never consider them as the responses of an intelligent spirit. This is the decided conviction of hundreds who have witnessed their performances in various parts of the country. Yet many have been, and others will be, deceived. And, doubtless, many tender and sensitive minds may be made insane by the wicked trifling of these unprincipled impostors. Certainly we have not the least desire to set at nought any thing of a *truly serious* character. Yet we are constrained to believe that the things of which we have spoken are too ridiculous and nonsensical, if not actually *sinful*, to be entitled to the least favor from the public. The learned Thomas Dick, in his Essay on the Improvement of Society, gives an account of far more singular and wonderful *phenomena* produced by *mechanical* agency, than any that has as yet been attributed to the agency of *spirits*, as affirmed by A. J. Davis, or La Roy Sunderland. And we here subjoin the facts of the case, for the benefit of the public:—

"Soon after the murder of King Charles I., a commission was appointed to survey the king's house at Woodstock, with the manor, park, and other demesnes belonging to that manor. One *Collins*, under a feigned name, hired himself as secretary to the commissioners, who, upon the 13th October, 1649, met, and took up their residence in the king's own rooms.

His majesty's bed chamber they made their kitchen, the council hall their pantry, and the presence chamber was the place where they met for the despatch of business. Things being thus prepared, they met on the 16th for business; and in the midst of their first debate, there entered a large *black dog* (as they thought,) which made a dreadful howling, overturned two or three of their chairs, and then crept under a bed and vanished. This gave them the greater surprise, as the doors were kept constantly locked, so that no real dog could get in or out. The next day their surprise was increased, when, sitting at dinner in a lower room, they heard plainly the noise of persons walking over their heads, though they well knew the doors were all locked, and there could be nobody there. Presently after, they heard, also, all the wood of the King's Oak brought by parcels from the dining room, and thrown with great violence into the presence chamber, as also all the chairs, stools, tables, and other furniture forcibly hurled about the room; their papers, containing the minutes of their transactions, were torn, and the ink glass broken. When all this noise had ceased, Giles Sharp, their secretary, proposed first to enter into these rooms; and in presence of the commissioners, from whom he received the key, he opened the doors, and found the wood spread about the room, the chairs tossed about and broken, the papers torn, but not the least track of any human creature, nor the least reason to suspect one, as the doors were all fast, and the keys in the custody of the commissioners. It was therefore unanimously agreed that the power that did this mischief must have entered at the key-hole. The night following, Sharp, with two of the commissioners' servants, as they were in bed in the same room, which room was contiguous to that where the commissioners lay, had their beds' feet lifted up so much higher than their heads, that they expected to have their necks broken, and then they were let fall at once with so much violence as shook the whole house, and more than ever terrified the commissioners. On the night of the 19th, as they were all in bed in the same room, for greater safety, and lights burning by them, the candles in an instant went out, with a sulphurous smell; and that moment many trenchers of wood were hurled about the room, which next morning were found to be the same their honors had eaten out of the day before, which were all removed from the pantry, though not a lock was found opened in the whole house. The next night they fared still worse; the candles went out, as before; the curtains of their honors' beds were rattled to and fro with great violence; they received many cruel blows and bruises by eight great pewter dishes and a number of wooden trenchers being thrown on their beds, which, being heaved off, were heard rolling about the room, though in the morning none of these were to be seen.

"The next night the keeper of the king's house and his dog lay in the commissioners' room, and then they had no disturbance. But on the night of the 22d, though the dog lay in the room as before, yet the candles went out, a number of brickbats fell from the chimney into the room, the dog howled piteously, their bed clothes were all stripped off, and their terror increased. On the 24th, they thought all the wood of the King's Oak was violently thrown down by their bedsides; they counted sixty-four billets that fell, and some hit and shook the beds in which they lay; but in the morning none was found there, nor had the door been opened where the billet wood was kept. The next night the candles were put out, the curtains rattled, and a dreadful crack, like thunder, was heard; and one of the servants, running in haste, thinking his master was killed, found three dozen of trenchers laid smoothly under the quilt by him. But all this was nothing to what succeeded afterwards. The 29th, about midnight, the candles went out; something walked majestically through the room, and opened and shut the windows; great stones were thrown violently into the room, some of which fell on the beds, others on the floor; and at about a quarter after one, a noise was heard as of forty cannon discharged together, and again repeated at about eight minutes' intervals. This alarmed and raised all the neighborhood, who, coming into their honors' room, gathered up the great stones, fourscore in number, and laid them by in the corner of a field, where they were afterwards to be seen. This noise, like the discharge of cannon, was heard for several miles round. During these noises, the commissioners and their servants gave one another over for lost, and cried out for help; and Giles Sharp, snatching up a sword, had well nigh killed one of their honors, mistaking him for the spirit, as he came in his shirt from his own room to theirs. While they were together, the noise was continued, and part of the tiling of the house was stripped off, and all the windows of an upper room were taken away with it. On the 30th, at midnight, something walked into the chamber, treading like a bear; it walked many times about, then threw the warming pan violently on the floor; at the same time, a large quantity of broken glass, accompanied with great stones and horse bones, came pouring into the room with uncommon force. On the 1st of November, the most dreadful scene of all ensued. Candles in every part of the room were lighted up, and a great fire made; at midnight, the candles all yet burning, a noise like the bursting of a cannon was heard in the room, and the burning billets were tossed about by it even into their honors' beds, who called Giles and his companions to their relief, otherwise the house had been burned to the ground; about an hour after, the candles went out as usual, the crack as of many cannon was heard, and many pailfuls of green stinking water were thrown upon their honors' beds; great stones were also thrown in as before, the bed curtains and bedsteads torn and broken, the windows shattered, and the whole neighborhood alarmed with the most dreadful noises; nay, the very rabbit stealers, that were abroad that night in the warren, were so terrified, that they fled for fear, and left their ferrets behind them. One of their honors this night spoke, and, *in the name of God, asked what it was, and why it disturbed them so.* No answer was given to this; but the noise ceased for a while, when the spirit came again; and as they all agreed, *brought with it seven devils worse than itself.* One of the servants now lighted a large candle, and set it in the doorway between the two chambers, to see what passed; and as he watched it, he plainly saw a hoof striking the candle and candlestick into the middle of the room, and afterwards, making three scrapes over the snuff, scraped it out. Upon this the same person was so bold as to draw a sword; but he had scarcely got it out, when he felt another invisible hand holding it too, and pulling it from him, and at length, prevailing, struck him so violently on the head with the pommel, that he fell down for dead with the blow. At this instant was heard another burst, like the discharge of the broadside of a ship of war, and at the interval of a minute or two between each, no less than nineteen such discharges. These shook the house so violently that they expected every moment it would fall upon their heads. The neighbors, being all alarmed, flocked to the house in great numbers, and all joined in prayer and psalm singing; during which the noise continued in the other rooms, and the discharge of cannons was heard as from without, though no visible agent was seen to discharge them. But what was the most alarming of all, and put an end to their proceedings effectually, happened the next day, as they were all at dinner, when a paper, in which they had signed a mutual agreement to reserve a part of the premises out of the general survey, and afterwards to share it equally among themselves, (which paper they had hid for the present under the earth, in a pot in one corner of the room, and in which an orange tree grew,) was consumed in a wonderful manner by the earth's taking fire, with which the pot was filled, and burning violently with a blue flame and an intolerable stench, so that they were all driven out of the house, to which they could never be again prevailed upon to return."

This story has been somewhat abridged from the Encyclopædia Britannica, where it is quoted from Dr. Plot's History of Oxfordshire, in which these extraordinary occurrences are ascribed to satanic influence. At the time they happened, they were viewed as the effects of *supernatural powers*; and even Dr. Plot seems disposed to ascribe them to this cause. "Though many tricks," says the doctor, "have often been played in affairs of this kind, yet many of the things above related are not reconcilable with juggling; such as the loud noises beyond the powers of man to make without such instruments as were not there; the tearing and breaking the beds; the throwing about the fire; the hoof treading out the candle; and the striving for the sword; and the blow the man received from the pommel of it." It was at length ascertained, however, that this wonderful contrivance was all the invention of the memorable Joseph Collins, of Oxford, otherwise called *Funny Joe*, who, having hired himself as secretary under the name of *Giles*

Sharp, by knowing the private traps belonging to the house, and by the help of *pulvis fulminans*, and other chemical preparations, and letting his fellow-servants into the scheme, carried on the deceit without discovery, to the very last.

The occurrences which are said to have taken place at the house of the Rev. Dr. Phelps, in Stratford, Connecticut, are not to be compared in their marvellousness to those we have quoted from Dr. Dick, and which things were the results of the *ingenuity of Joe Collins*. Therefore, when we hear of such like occurrences in our day, there will be no necessity for us to attribute them to any supernatural influence, either good or bad; for it is a well-received maxim, that "*what man has done man can do*." To suppose that the merciful *Father* of *spirits* would harass and frighten mankind by haunting their houses with strange noises and rappings, ghosts and hobgoblins, and spirits of the uneasy dead, would be derogatory to his paternal character. And who, for a moment, could believe that he would torment little children in this way, when our Savior took them in his arms, and blessed them, and said, "Of such is the kingdom of heaven"? No, we must attribute such things to any other source than as proceeding from the throne of God.

Up to the present time it may be that many will profess to the world that they have actually seen the spirits of the departed. Yet this is no new profession, for the votaries of St. Vitus, and the spiritually-minded Shakers of later times, have declared to us that they have seen their departed friends and acquaintances. But even Mr. Davis is led to consider a large majority of these cases to be the results of cerebral agitation. "I can truthfully affirm," says he, "that the objects, localities, scenery, and personages, seen by those laboring under monomania, delirium tremens, &c., are of the same class of mental delusion, and are absolutely nothing more than the unconscious elaborations of the surcharged brain."

CHAPTER XVI.

EVIL EFFECTS OF POPULAR SUPERSTITIONS.

The following are some of the evils that result from a belief in popular superstitions:—

1. They have caused a great waste of time. Look at the practice of heathen nations. Their religious ceremonies are altogether superstitious. All the time devoted to false gods must be considered as wasted. Take a survey, too, of Catholic countries. During the dark ages, their priests were engaged in nonsensical disputes. Treatise after treatise was composed on such subjects as the following: How many angels can stand on the point of a needle? Have spirits any navels? Is the Virgin Mary the mother of God? and a thousand others equally senseless and unprofitable. In their monasteries, multitudes passed their days in repeating unintelligible prayers, poring over the legends of their saints, cutting figures in paper, and tormenting their bodies for the good of their souls. Turn our attention to Protestant lands, and here we find, also, that many a folio has been written on foolish and unintelligible subjects; that many a day has been occupied in trying and burning witches and heretics; that many a pharasaic custom has been scrupulously observed, and many an absurd opinion advanced and defended. Even in our own times, many hours are occupied in discoursing about dreams and visions, signs and tricks, spectres and apparitions; in consulting charms and lots, and fortune tellers; in prying into future events and occurrences; in borrowing trouble on account of some supposed unfavorable omen; or in various other practices equally vain and superstitious. Now, all this is wrong. Time is given for no such purposes. We have but a short period allotted to us to remain in this world, and a great work to accomplish. Let us then be always engaged in something useful and virtuous.

2. Popular superstitions have caused a great waste of human life. Cast your eye over the page of history. You there notice an account of the trial by ordeal. The accused person was required either to hold red-hot iron balls in his naked hands, or to walk over red-hot plates of iron with bare feet. If he escaped unburned, he was considered innocent; but if he was scorched, sentence of death was pronounced. Or he was compelled either to thrust his arm into a caldron of boiling water, or be thrown into a deep pond. If he was either unscalded or drowned, his innocence was proved; but if he was scalded or could swim, the sentence of condemnation was passed. In neither case could life be saved, except by the interposition of a miracle;

and this was not expected on such occasions. And through this superstition, thousands perished in the most cruel and unrighteous manner. A distinguished writer computes that more than one hundred thousand persons, of all ages, have suffered death for witchcraft alone. Only think! one hundred thousand persons murdered for a crime of which no human person was ever guilty!

There are others who bring upon themselves sickness, and even death, by their belief in signs, dreams, and forewarnings. But as the gospel sheds abroad its divine light, these things are found to recede, and to give place to more rational views of divine wisdom and goodness, in the control and arrangement of events having a relation to our being and happiness. The author of the Family Encyclopædia says, that "the superstitious notions of ghosts, spirits, &c., are rapidly declining; and notwithstanding all the solemn tales which have been propagated, there is no reason to believe that any real spirits or celestial agents have held intercourse with man since the establishment of Christianity;" and that "the history of modern miracles, appearances of the dead, &c., will be always found, when thoroughly examined, merely the phantoms of a disordered imagination."

3. Popular superstitions have caused great and unnecessary misery. We need not refer to history for an illustration of this assertion. We have sufficient examples around us. Look into society, and we shall find one class who pay particular attention to all signs and dreams. If any thing unfavorable is indicated, their feelings are greatly depressed; and if the contrary, they are as much elated. If a little insect, called the death watch, knocks for its mate on the wall, sleepless nights are sure to follow. If they notice the new moon over the wrong shoulder, their comfort is destroyed for a whole month. Nanny Scott, the old washerwoman, is sure that another death will happen in the family this year, because, when her sister-in-law was taken out to be buried, somebody shut the door before the corpse was under ground, and so shut death into the house. And her neighbor, the good Mrs. Taylor, suffers the baby to scratch and disfigure its face, because it is said to be unlucky to cut the nails of a child under a year old. Another neighbor has seen a single raven fly over the house, or heard a cricket chirping upon the hearth, and is greatly alarmed, because such things are said to be a sign of death to some member of the family within the year. And thus many are found who are silly enough to imbitter their own lives and the lives of others by such foolish superstitions.

There may be noticed another class, whose belief in the supernatural origin of signs, omens, and warnings leads them to adopt measures for their speedy fulfilment. Many a wedded couple seem to think they must quarrel because it happened to storm on the day they were married; and when some dispute arises between them, they fall to fighting, to prove, if possible, the truth of the prediction. And for all this interruption of domestic harmony, they blame, not their own tempers and passions, but the decrees of fate. Many a person has concluded he must live in poverty all his days, because a few moles have appeared on the wrong side of his body. And hence he neglects all industry and economy, and dissipates his time, his privileges, and his talents.

We may notice a third class, who give themselves to tricks, fortune telling, and opening books, to discover the events of futurity. Their spirits vary with the supposed indications of good or evil occurrences. "A lady, who moved in the first circles, was once visiting in a clergyman's family of my acquaintance," says the late Rev. Bernard Whitman, "and it was her regular morning custom to toss up a little box of pins, and make her happiness for the day depend upon their accidental variation in falling. If they came down more heads than points, she was cheerful and happy; but if more points than heads, she was gloomy and wretched. It seemed she valued her comfort, worth at least a brass pin." Many a worthy Christian has not only been deprived of his happiness, but betrayed into wild, extravagant, and even sinful acts, by attempting to follow the suggestion of the passage which first meets his eye on opening the Bible. Many a poor wight has formed a disadvantageous matrimonial alliance, because some old hag has described black eyes and rosy cheeks as the characteristics of his future bride.

We may notice, moreover, a fourth class, who are forever anticipating some dreadful calamity. Let any fool solemnly proclaim that war, famine, or pestilence is approaching, and they will give more heed to it than to that holy word which assures us that our heavenly Father will never leave nor forsake us. All uncommon appearances in the heavens they look upon as indications of the threatened judgments of an angry God. Even the beautiful Aurora Borealis, which spans the blue concave above us, was so interpreted. To permit such fears to disturb and destroy our happiness is a sin against Heaven. Our heavenly Father created us for enjoyment. He has furnished us with capacities and means of felicity. He has even commanded us to rejoice in the Lord always. He has given us a religion to effect this desirable object. It is as much a part of this religion to be always cheerful, contented, and happy, as to be always temperate, just, and virtuous. And if people would take one tenth part of the pains to make themselves happy that they do to render themselves miserable, there would be ten times the present amount of happiness. "By the grace of God," says the Rev. John Wesley, "I never fret. I repine at nothing; I am discontented at nothing. And to have persons at my ear fretting and murmuring at every thing is like tearing the flesh from off my bones. I see God sitting upon his throne, and ruling all things well." A companion of Mr. Wesley says that he never saw him low-spirited in his life, nor could he endure to be with an unhappy, melancholic person. "Every believer," he often remarked, "should enjoy life." "I dare no more fret," said he, "than curse or swear." Would that all Christians were as cheerful and consistent as Mr. Wesley. There would be less of dark and dismal forebodings; less of distrust, and more of solid peace and comfort, in the soul. It seems that Melancthon was somewhat of a melancholic turn of mind, and, when gloomy and dejected, would call upon Luther, and relate to him his troubles and afflictions. Luther, being of a more lively and hopeful turn, after listening to him a short time, would jump upon his feet, and say, "Come, come, let us sing the forty-sixth psalm;" and when they had sung that, all was peaceful and happy again.

As to what is commonly termed good or ill luck, we may be assured that they have no other existence but in the imagination. Luck means chance; but every thing, great and small, is under the wise and gracious direction of God. Nothing can happen without his permission, and he permits nothing but what, in his wonderful plans, he designs to work for our good. We are kept in ignorance of the particular events that are to befall us, in order to keep alive within us an abiding sense of our dependence on God, and a constant obedience to the directions of his word, by which alone we can be prepared to meet the dispensations of his providence. The Bible tells us quite enough of futurity to teach us to prepare for it, as far as it rests with us to prepare. And it is both vain and wicked to endeavor to obtain any further information from any other source, or for any one to pretend that they possess it. Had it been necessary for our good that we should know every thing beforehand, the information would have been given us in the Bible, or it would have been left so that we could have gathered it from general instruction and observation, as is the case with every kind of knowledge that is essential to our present as well as everlasting good. It certainly would not have been left to creaking doors, croaking ravens, or ill-made tallow candles. Neither would God reveal to weak and wicked men or women the designs of his providence, which no human wisdom is able to foresee. To consult these false oracles is not only foolish, but sinful. It is foolish, because they themselves are as ignorant as those whom they pretend to teach; and it is sinful, because it is prying into that futurity which God, in mercy, as well as in wisdom, hides from man. God indeed orders all things; but when you have a mind to do a foolish thing, do not fancy that you are *fated* to do it; this is tempting Providence, not trusting God. It is charging him with folly. Prudence is his gift, and you obey him better when you make use of prudence, under the direction of prayer, than when you heedlessly rash into ruin, and think you are only submitting to your fate. Fancy never that you are compelled to undo yourself, or to rush upon your own destruction, in compliance with any supposed fatality. Believe never that God conceals his will from a sober Christian, who obeys his laws, and reveals it to a vagabond, who goes from place to place, breaking the laws both of God and man. King Saul never consulted the witch until he left off serving God. The Bible will direct us best. Conjurers are impostors; and there are no days unlucky but those we make so by our vanity, folly, and sin.

4. Popular superstitions have greatly injured the cause of medicine. That superstition which leads people to believe in the efficacy of charms is very injurious. We will enumerate a few cases by way of example. The scrofula, for instance, is frequently called the *king's evil.* It received this name because it was generally believed that the touch of a king would cure the disorder. For centuries this belief was so prevalent, that any one who should call it in question would have been considered no less than an infidel, and an enemy to his king and country. And so great was the demand for the king's touch, from invalids, that one day in seven was set apart for the king to bestow healing mercies on his subjects. Vast numbers flocked to him, from Wales, Ireland, Scotland, and many parts of the continent. An exact register was kept of the number of persons who came to Charles the Second for relief, from 1660 to 1664, and they amounted to twenty-three thousand six hundred and one. From May, 1667, to 1684, the number of persons touched amounted to sixty-eight thousand five hundred and six. Total, ninety-two thousand one hundred and seven. The practice was begun in the year 1051, and continued until the reign of the present royal family, who were possessed of too much sense to encourage such an idle superstition. But notwithstanding this belief and practice were abandoned by the royal family, yet, with some individuals, a belief still prevails that certain persons are endowed with healing power.

In 1807, a farmer in Devonshire, England, who was the ninth son of a ninth son, officiated in the cure of the king's evil, and multitudes believed that they received healing from his touch. In this country, a *seventh* son of a seventh son has officiated in similar cases, and performed incredible cures, as we are told by those who think they have received signal blessings through his instrumentality.

Not many years since, the cold hands of a convict, who had terminated his life on the gallows, in Liverpool, were drawn over several wens a number of times to effect a cure. A person in one of our western states ran a pitchfork into his hand, and he applied a plaster to the cold iron as well as to the fresh wound. When people run a nail into their foot, they frequently save and polish the rusty iron to facilitate the recovery. Some time since, in the State of Maine, the body of a female was taken from the grave, her heart taken out, dried, and pulverized, and given to another member of the family, as a specific against the consumption. And the same thing has more recently been done in the town of Waltham, Massachusetts. The heart was reduced to a powder, and made into pills, but they did not cure the patient; while the person who took up the remains from the grave, and removed the heart, came very near losing his life, from the putrefactive state of the corpse at the time.

We could relate many other cases, equally foolish and disgusting. All such things should be classed under the general name of charms, and be looked upon as relics of the grossest superstitions. Why not as well have the touch of a slave as a king? Why not as well apply your plaster to a tree as to a pitchfork? Why not as well drink the heart of a lamb as a woman? You may say that God has determined certain cures shall follow certain applications. No such determination is published in his word, and no such conclusions can be inferred from facts. You may pretend that a special miracle is wrought in such cases. But this is incredible; for the object is not compatible with the miraculous interposition of Deity. And the few cures which are reputed to have taken place can be satisfactorily accounted for, on the influence of the imagination, and other natural causes. So that such a belief is not only superstitious, but calculated to lead people to neglect the proper means of recovery, and thus injure themselves and the medical profession.

In the years 1808, '9, and '10, a Mr. Austin of Colchester, Vermont, gave out that he was a gifted person in the art of healing; and if the patient would describe to him, by word of mouth, or by letter, the true symptoms of his malady, he would receive healing at his word, if indeed his disease was curable. In a very little time the obscure retreat of Austin was thronged with invalids, coming from almost every section of the country; and Colchester was scarcely less in favor than Ballston or Saratoga. The mail carriers groaned under the burden of maladies described. Bar rooms at public inns, on roads leading to Colchester, were decorated with letters directed to the "Prophet of Colchester;" and vagrants were found travelling over the country, collecting of invalids their evil symptoms, to be truly and faithfully delivered to the prophet in a given time, at the moderate price of fifty cents per letter. We were soon referred to cases wherein the most inveterate deafness was removed; the blind saw; dropsies and consumptions, in the last stages of them, were cured; and the patient, it is said, in many instances, would tell the day and the hour when their letters were received by the prophet, although they might be some hundred miles distant from the deliverer, because, at such an hour, they began to mend. The prophet, however, did not long enjoy his far-famed celebrity. His house, after a while, was deserted of invalids. The people discovered their folly, and permitted him to sink into his former merited obscurity. It was just the same with the celebrated *rain-water* doctor, as he was called, who established himself at one time in Providence, and at another time in the vicinity of Boston. Many of those now living can recollect the accounts of marvellous cures, and the flocking of invalids of all descriptions to his temple of health. But the community at length discovered the imposition of his practice, and left him to the undisturbed enjoyment of his rain water and his gruel.

The most recent case of medical imposition practised upon the public, that has come to our knowledge, is that of a practitioner in New York city, who, by receiving a letter from sick or diseased persons, giving the year, day, and hour of their birth, immediately forwards them a package of medicine suited to their case. It seems to be a matter of astonishment to many how he arrives at a knowledge of their state of health, so as to be able to adapt his remedies to their several conditions. But it is probably done on the principles of astrology—by finding the planet under which the patient is born, the diseases appertaining to that planet, and the *plants* belonging to the same, which are supposed to have a special effect upon the relative *planetary* diseases. Culpepper, in his English Herbal, if we mistake not, arranges or classifies all plants and diseases in this way, and contends that astrology is the only true key to medical science. Fortune telling is practised upon a similar plan, through the agency of *astrology*. But the whole is a deception, entirely unworthy the age in which we live. The fortune teller may hit upon an incident which is correct, once in a while, and it would be strange if he did not. And the *astrological physician* may prescribe some little tonic, or stimulant, that will raise the drooping spirits for a time, and actually lead the hopeful patient to believe that he or she is fast recovering from their long-afflictive maladies. But the sequel too often teaches them the lesson of their sad mistake.

The history of Valentine Greataks, the son of an Irish gentleman, who lived in the time of Cromwell, is very similar to what we have related of the prophet of Colchester. And about the same time, Francisco Bagnone, a Capuchin friar, was famous in Italy, having a gift of healing, principally by his hands only. Multitudes of sick people attended him wherever he went, to obtain healing mercy. And here, perhaps, we may find the true principle on which all the impositions of Popery have been maintained for centuries gone by. It cannot be a matter of surprise that, if men, of more information than they, can be made to believe that they are delivered from disease by experiments of magnetism, tractors, or the mere touch of the hand, these should believe that they are healed by visiting the tombs of saints; by standing before their statues; being touched by nails from their coffins, rings from their fingers, or by the bones of the fingers themselves.

We are by no means authorized to say that none of these persons were relieved of pains and diseases by seeking relief in this way. So great is the influence of the imagination on the nervous, vascular, and muscular systems, as has already been shown, that it would be no more than probable that obstructions, causing pain and sickness, should in some instances be removed, and lay a foundation for recovery. And, moreover, that in a still greater number of instances the power of the imagination on the origin of the nerves within the brain should counteract the motion to the brain by disease acting upon the extremities of the nerves; and thus the patient for a season might experience relief from pain, and even feel pleasure, as was the case with an artist upon the Pont Royal, mentioned by Dr. Sigault, and in the gambols of the rheumatic patient, as mentioned by Dr. Haygarth. But in all these cases, experiment and illustration, like those of the commissioners at Paris, and like that of Dr. Haygarth in England, would disclose the real ground of these effects. The patients would no longer attribute them to a supernatural influence. They would learn why, in most cases, the relief supposed to be obtained was only momentary, and why all those gifted persons, both in Europe and America, have had no more than an ephemeral celebrity, and, in most instances, lived to see themselves neglected, and their pretensions become the subjects of just satire and reproof.

5. Popular superstitions have greatly injured the cause of religion. That superstition which allows any substitute for personal holiness is very pernicious. The Pharisees considered themselves holy, because they were the descendants of faithful Abraham. They fasted twice a week; paid tithes of all they possessed; made long prayers in public places; and were strict observers of all sacred days and religious ceremonies. At the same time, they neglected the weightier matters of the law—justice, mercy, faithfulness; devoured widows' houses; were proud, bigoted, and self-righteous.

Some people think they lived only in the times of the apostles. "But we should recollect," says the Rev. George Whitefield, "that vipers and toads have the most eggs, and most numerous progeny. If you were to look at the eggs of a toad through a microscope, you would be surprised at the innumerable multitude; and the Pharisees are an increasing generation of vipers, which hatch and spread all over the world. If you would know a Pharisee, he is one who pretends to endeavor, and talks about keeping the law of God, and does not know its spirituality. There are some of them very great men, in their own estimation, and frequently make the greatest figure in the church. One of them, a gentleman's son, because he had not broken the letter of the law, thought he was right and without sin. "O," says he, "if I have nothing to do but to keep the commandments, I am safe. I have honored my father and mother; I never stole; what need he to steal who has so good an estate? I never committed adultery." No, no! he loved his character too well for that: but our Lord opens to him the law—*This one thing thou lackest; go, sell all thou hast, and give to the poor:* he loved his money more than his God; Christ brought him back to the first commandment, though he catechized him first in the fifth. So Paul was a Pharisee. He says, '*I was alive without the law, once; I was, touching the law, blameless.*" How can that be? Can a man be without the law, and yet, touching the law, be blameless? Says he, "I was without the law; that is, I was not brought to see its spirituality. I thought myself a very good man." No man could say of Paul, Black is his eye. "But," says he, "when God brought the commandment with power upon my soul, then I saw my specks, and beheld my lack of true righteousness."

Some Roman Catholics perform tedious pilgrimages; lacerate their own bodies; abstain from meats on certain days; and some have paid the pope or priests for the pardon of their sins, or purchased indulgences for the commission of wickedness. Some Protestants, too, attend punctually upon all religious meetings, subscribe liberally to the charities of the day, observe all gospel ordinances, and profess great attachment to the cause of Christ; and yet are fretful, unkind, and disobliging in their families; censorious in their conversation; uncharitable in their judgment; grasping in their dealings, and unhappy in their dispositions. Some have thought that, because Christ died for the sins of the whole world they could commit sin with impunity; or, if they were elected, they could do what they pleased, and be sure of heaven at last. But all these things have no foundation in reason, experience, or revelation, and may therefore be considered superstitious. A belief in them is exceedingly injurious to the cause of piety and holiness, because it leads to the neglect of the one thing needful—a uniformly sober, righteous, and godly life. God will certainly render unto every man according to his deeds. Be he Pharisee or Sadducee, Catholic or Protestant, elect or non-elect, he can escape the punishment of no sin but by repentance and reformation. And no sin is ever removed, no virtue is ever given, by miracle. Our iniquities must be forsaken, and our goodness acquired, by our own exertions, aided by the promised influence of the Holy Spirit. And, until we have accomplished these ends, we cannot rationally expect pure and permanent happiness.

There have been opinions respecting the devil, tinctured somewhat with superstition, that have contributed to bring reproach upon the Scriptures, which were supposed to teach the existence of just such a being as many believed him to be. Martin Luther, in speaking of his confinement in the castle of Wartburg, says, "The people brought me, among other things, some hazel nuts, which I put into a box, and sometimes I used to crack and eat of them. In the night time, my gentleman, the devil, came and got the nuts out of the box, and cracked them against one of the bed posts, making a very great noise and rumbling about my bed; but I regarded him nothing at all: when afterwards I began to slumber, then he kept such a racket and rumbling upon the chamber stairs, as if many empty barrels and hogsheads had been tumbling down."

Dr. Cotton Mather, in the time of New England witchcraft, took home one of the possessed damsels, to learn the ways and works of Satan. When the doctor called the family to prayers, she would whistle, and sing, and yell, to drown his voice, would strike at him with her fist, and try to kick him. But her hand or foot would always recoil when within an inch or two of his body; thus giving the idea that there was a sort of invisible coat of mail, of heavenly temper, and proof against the assaults of the devil, around his sacred person. She seemed to be greatly displeased at the thought of his making public the doings of her master, the evil one; and when he attempted to write a sermon against him, she would disturb and interrupt him all manner of ways. For instance, she once knocked at his study door, and said that there was somebody down stairs that would be glad to see him; he dropped his pen, and went down: upon entering the room he found no one there but his own family. He afterwards undertook to chide her for having told a falsehood. She denied that she told a falsehood. "Did not you say that there was somebody down stairs that would be glad to see me?" "Well," she replied, with great pertness, "is not Mrs. Mather always glad to see you?" She even went much further than this in persecuting the good man while he was writing his sermon: she threw large books at his head. But he struggled manfully at these buffetings of Satan, as he considered them to be, finished the sermon, related all these and other kindred circumstances in it, preached and published it. Richard Baxter wrote the preface to an edition printed in London, in which he declares that "he who will not be convinced, by the evidence Dr. Mather presents, that the child was bewitched, must be a very obdurate Sadducee."

A few years since, a house in Maine was said to be haunted. The building and furniture were shaken, dreadful noises were heard, dismal sights were seen, and heavy blows were received. The occupant of the house had lately left a Calvinistic theological seminary. He afterwards became a settled Universalist preacher. "A neighboring family informed me," says the late Bernard Whitman, "that he now considered it the Spirit of God, haunting him to forsake Calvinism, and proclaim universal salvation." His explanation, though satisfactory to himself, may not be equally so to our readers.

The devil should never be made a packhorse for our sins, nor should our thoughts be turned from within, causing us to neglect a watch upon our own lusts and passions, in looking for the assaults of some outward tempter. The effect sometimes produced upon the minds of children has a very unfavorable influence. A pious mother, not finding it convenient to attend her little son to rest, told him to omit his prayers for one night. "Mother," said the child, "will the devil forgive me if I neglect my prayers?"

"What shall we say," says the late Professor Stuart, "of the excessive use that has been made of the passages that speak of his influence and dominion? Because, in reference to the wide-spread influence of Satan, he is called the 'prince of this world,' and even the 'god of this world,' are we *literally* to interpret passages of this nature, and thus in a clandestine manner introduce effectually the old dualism of Zoroaster and the Persians? This, indeed, has often, very often, been substantially done; done, I acknowledge, for the most part without any direct intention of such a nature. Still there is an impression, wide spread among the lower classes of people, even in our own country, that Satan is a kind of omnipotent being; and he is often represented as the successful, or rather the invincible, rival of the great Redeemer.

"Yet the New Testament is full enough of instruction relative to this subject to correct any erroneous views in relation to it, if it be duly examined. I need only appeal to the large class of passages which represent Satan as a conquered enemy; as 'falling like lightning from heaven;' as being reduced to a state of impotence in respect to that deadly power which he exercises, (Heb. ii. 14;) and all the evil principalities, and powers, and magistrates (1 Cor. xv. 24, Eph. vi. 12, Col. ii. 15) as being subdued, or to be subdued and utterly discomfited, by Christ; for 'the prince of this world is cast out,' (John xii. 31;) 'the Son of God was manifested that he might destroy the works of the devil,' (1 John iii. 8;) and Christians are every where spoken of as being liberated from his dominion and power, (1 John v. 18-44.) When the apostle, therefore, calls Satan 'the god of this world,' and the Savior calls him 'the prince of this world,' it is the world of the wicked which is meant; for such is the usual idiom of the Scriptures. And as to the power of Satan over the wicked, it is every where presented in the New Testament as something that will wholly cease after a time, and the reign of the Prince of Peace become universal.

"How deeply these considerations intrench upon the long-practised methods of exhibiting Satan as omnipotent and omnipresent every thinking mind will easily perceive. Especially has the Romish church erred here beyond all bounds of reason or moderation. According to the doctrines which they sedulously inculcate, Satan has not only irresistible power over the world of the wicked, but, next to such a power, even over Christians. Nothing but exorcisms, and holy chrisms, and lustrations with holy water, and incantations, and the like, can keep off evil spirits, or disarm them of their fatal power. And as the consummation and chief end of all the doctrine, nothing short of the interposition of the priesthood can secure any one against destruction, either in this world or the next—an interposition, however, which is not *freely given*, as the Savior commanded the disciples to impart the blessings of the gospel, but to be purchased at whatever price the church may fix upon it."—*Bibliotheca Sacra*, February, 1843.

Language sometimes used in times of excitement is prejudicial to the cause of religion. It is sometimes said that the Almighty is visiting such a town; that he is coming this way; that he has taken up his abode in a certain village; that he will remain but a few days; that he has been driven away by unbelievers, and that he cannot be expected again for some months or years. Now, it should be remembered that God is every where present, and that his spirit is always striving within the soul; and its voice is drowned only by the strife and tumult of our own discordant passions. The Spirit is ever ready to assist us, whenever we resolve to use our own efforts in hearty coöperation. And if revivals of religion seem to be of a *periodical* nature, it is because our own zeal or engagedness is too fitful. The church can enjoy a constant season of refreshing from the presence of the Lord, only let its members be ever active, ever diligent, ever devoted and persevering. God works not by miracle, but through the agency of common means or efforts. We must not, therefore, defer attention to the duties of religion, in expectation of some special interposition of Heaven. We should remember that a sober, righteous, and godly life is the best evidence of true conversion; and that we are called upon *to work out our own salvation* with fear and trembling, God himself having vouchsafed to work within us both to will and to do of his good pleasure.

CHAPTER XVII.

BANISHMENT OF POPULAR SUPERSTITIONS.

Seeing the evils of popular superstitions, what course shall we adopt for their banishment? Or, in other words, how shall we best lend a helping hand to hasten the downfall of ignorance, error, and sin?

1. We must deliver ourselves from their domination; for we are all more or less under their influence. When any of the common signs of good or evil fortune appear before us, our thoughts involuntarily recur to the thing supposed to be signified. Sometimes a momentary shudder is communicated to the whole system; unpleasant sensations are often excited; and frequently a depression of spirits is produced. And how can we free ourselves from this thraldom? By the exercise of our reason. A proper use of our reasoning faculties will enable us to accomplish this undertaking. We must endeavor to convince ourselves that all these things are the offspring of ignorance; that they have no foundation in reason, philosophy, or religion; and that they are exceedingly pernicious in their consequences. When fully persuaded of these truths, we must strive to make our feelings coincide with the dictates of our understandings. And this we can effect by persevering self-discipline. Such exertions, with the blessing of Heaven, will eventually deliver us from the inconvenience, vexation, and slavery of popular superstitions. And as such a consummation is most ardently to be desired, we must enter upon the duty with a zeal and earnestness commensurate with its importance.

2. We must also assist our fellow-men in the performance of this great and good work. When we meet with those who believe in ghosts, in signs, enchantments, and divination, we must try to persuade them that no dependence whatever can be placed on any of these vanities—that they are all fictions, absurdities, and abominations. And perhaps, in some cases, if we cannot produce conviction by sober sense and sound argument, we may be justified in resorting to ridicule.

It is a lamentable consideration that so much time should be criminally wasted in many families in explaining tricks, relating and expounding dreams, telling fortunes, and in detailing stories of haunted houses, hobgoblins, and spirits of the supposed uneasy dead. In this way, the evil is cherished, and transmitted from generation to generation. But if we can succeed in giving an opposite direction to conversation; if we can induce people to reason upon these things, and inquire into their origin, causes, and effects, and investigate the evidence on which they are imagined to rest, and adopt rational conclusions, we shall be usefully employed. A course like this would eventually lead to the banishment of popular superstitions, with their baneful effects upon our peace and happiness; especially if we labor to impress upon the minds of others the existence of an all-wise Providence, that controls and governs all things for the highest good of all, calling upon us to place our trust in Him, without whose notice not even a sparrow falleth to the ground.

3. We must likewise attend to the early education of our children. It is during infancy and childhood that our heads are filled with "nursery tales" and marvellous stories. They are told us by those to whose care we are early intrusted, either to frighten us into obedience, to gratify our thirst for the new and wonderful, or to while away a tedious evening. They sink into our confiding hearts, and leave impressions the most pernicious and the most lasting. Could a child be educated without any knowledge of such things, he would never be troubled with their baneful influence. Our duty is therefore plain. In taking the principal care of our children at home, we should not permit them to learn any such things from our own lips; and we should evince, too, by our daily conduct, that they exert no influence on our own feelings, character, or happiness. In intrusting our offspring in early life to the care of other persons, we must charge them, as faithful guardians of the young, to conceal every thing of the kind from their knowledge. And after our children become of sufficient age to associate with others, we must caution them to avoid believing or relating any superstitious tales as they would shun known falsehoods. By persevering in this course, we shall save them from the degrading influence of popular superstitions.

4. We must, moreover, endeavor to increase the means of public education. We generally find that the most enlightened are the most free from superstition; and it therefore follows that a high degree of mental cultivation will effect a general deliverance. And how shall this great object be accomplished? We must reason with them upon the immense value and importance of knowledge. We must show them, by an appeal to facts, that all our civil, social, domestic, and religious blessings depend on the intelligence and virtue of the people. But perhaps many will complain of the scarcity of money and the want of means. If so, we must also show them, by an appeal to incontrovertible facts, that more money is annually wasted, in all our towns, in extravagant living, dress, furniture, and equipage; squandered in shows, amusements, balls, and parties; in gaming, dissipation, public parades, and intoxicating liquors, than is expended for the instruction of the rising generation. No, there is not a lack of funds. Where there is a will there is also a way. The value and importance of the subject is not generally understood; or, if understood, is not properly

appreciated. Almost every thing else seems of more consequence than learning and wisdom. Yet this will never answer. The world is growing wiser. Those who will not employ the requisite means must rest contented with comparative ignorance. Let *us* not be of this unworthy number. If we feel the importance of the change in these respects, let us persevere in our laudable exertions, leaving no objections unanswered, no measures untried, until we succeed in giving our children a high degree of education. And if the Father of spirits shall see fit to prolong our lives to witness the results, we shall look upon the almost universal banishment of popular superstitions.

5. Finally, we must labor for the diffusion of pure and undefiled religion, adhering alone to the teachings of Jesus. We shall then believe in one perfect, all-pervading Spirit, who regulates all the events of this world which are above our control, and that all his various dispensations originate in perfect wisdom and goodness. We shall believe that we have no worse enemies than our own sinful lusts and passions, and that power is given us through faith to conquer these, even in this state of existence. We shall believe that it is as much our duty to be always happy as it is to be always honest and virtuous. We shall have the assurance that our heavenly Father has commissioned no fate nor chance, spectres nor devils, to torment us. And if we live up to this belief, we shall secure a large share of temporal enjoyment, and be prepared for the increased and increasing felicity of the spiritual world. If we produce this state of faith and practice in ourselves and in those around us, we shall have done much for the banishment of popular superstitions and the downfall of ignorance, error, and sin.

PART SECOND.

MIRACLE IN SPRINGFIELD, MASSACHUSETTS.

Four gentlemen in Springfield, not long since, publicly attested to a "miracle," performed, as they believed, by spirits, at a "circle" where they were present. It consisted in moving a table, and a number of chairs in the room, and in shocks, resembling distant thunder, or cannon at a distance, causing the persons and the chairs and tables to tremble in such a manner that the effects were both seen and felt, the room being well lighted at the time, and an opportunity afforded for the closest inspection, so that the company unitedly declare that *they know they were not imposed upon nor deceived.*

Now, there is nothing very remarkable in this affair, for all might have been done by the medium himself, by first pathetizing the persons present, as it might be done without their knowledge, and while in that state could be made to see and hear any thing imagined by the operator. We are assured, by one who knows, that it is impossible for those who are fit subjects to be present at a circle without being more or less under the mesmeric influence. And, in such cases, they can be *willed* to remember or forget what they have seen or heard. We do not consider such persons as competent witnesses in such a case as they have testified to. It may all have been induced, or it may all have been real. And if real, there was no need to refer it to the agency of spirits, since such things have been done without spirits, as in the case of Joe Collins, or others which we shall refer to, in this part of our volume. But here we may be told, that a thousand dollars has been offered to any one who will prove that such things are produced by any other power than that of *spirits.* But the same sum has been offered to any one who will prove that *spirits* move tables, chairs, and the like, or that *spirits* produce the noises and other manifestations ascribed to them.

We have heard the case of a person who went to a medium and wished to know if he could be put in communication with his father, who had died several years before. He was answered in the affirmative. But the inquirer desired, as proof that it would actually be the spirit of his father that would be introduced to him, that a pencil and paper should be laid upon a table, and that the spirit of the father should come and write his own name upon the paper, the son feeling assured that, if this were done, he should at once recognize both the name and the writing. Accordingly, the spirit in question came, and did as was desired, and the son declared it to be the real name and handwriting of his father. Now, the philosophy of the case is this: The inquirer was first pathetized, although ignorant of the fact at the time—a thing very common, though not generally understood. Thus the medium became acquainted with the name of the father as it existed in the mind of the son; but did the pencil actually write the name upon the paper? No. It was only made to *appear* so to the mind of the inquirer. As to the handwriting, the inquirer's mind was directed to a piece of paper, and to look at the writing. Of course, he saw his father's name, and the handwriting, for he could see nothing else for the time being, his mind being impressed with that one idea or object, and closed to every thing else. It was in fact, to him, his father's name and chirography, and no one's else. It could not be otherwise while his mind was under the control of the operator.

We have been told of a lady, who, in a magnetized state, sits at a table and writes down information that is imparted to her, as is said, from the world of spirits. Her hand and pen glide over the paper with astonishing speed and velocity, far more rapid than the most expert penman in a normal state. And what astonishes many is, that she cannot stop writing when she wishes to, and sometimes becomes so exceedingly fatigued as to beg of the spirit or spirits to grant her a little repose from the wearisome task. But the whole matter is easily accounted for, without referring it to the supposed agency of spirits. The lady's arm is first paralyzed—deprived of motion by the will of the medium or operator, so that her own mind or will has not the least control over it. She thus becomes a mere machine, under the will and control of another, whose will directs the movements of the arm and pen, and dictates what is written in answer to inquiries made of things appertaining to the spirit world, just as Miss Martineau declares, in her letters on magnetism, that "the volitions of the mesmerist may actuate the movements of the patient's limbs, and suggest the material of his ideas." Many singular effects are produced upon the minds and feelings of subjects in a sleep-waking state, by Professor Williams, Dr. Cutter, and others, such as being made drunk with water, eating cayenne as sugar, exercising complete control over their mental as well as physical condition.

We have been assured by a pathetist, who is a thorough adept in the profession, that he *can* and often *has* put persons in communication *apparently* with a deceased father, mother, brother, sister, or friend. The individual is first *pathetized* (another name for mesmerism) by him in a wakeful state, though unconscious, it may be, that he is under such an influence. His mind being in the possession and under the control of the operator, a person is now either actually or mentally (for it makes no difference) presented before him, and he is told of the fact, and asked, *Do you not see your father?* The idea of *father* is so presented to the mind, through the organ of *form*, that the organ can take cognizance of none other than the father. The *person*, if an actual person is employed for the occasion, is then shifted or changed for another person; yet the subject perceives no difference, even if changed successively for a dozen others; it is all the same; it is *father*, and no one else, through the whole exhibition. The father speaks, the son recognizes his voice, and they converse together. The subject can be willed to hear any sound, as that of music, artillery, thunder, and the like, though no sounds whatever are in reality made. A niece of ours was operated on in this way, and she was told to look abroad and behold the majestic waves of the ocean, the pageantry of a military procession; and she saw and was delighted with the scenes that were *willed* to pass before her. Apples were oranges to her, and she sucked their juice with a delightful zest. An apple paring held before her was a beautiful bird, then a squirrel, a rabbit, or whatever the operator *willed* it to become. The mind of the operator and the subject, in such cases, become as one, and they then hear, see, taste, and feel the same thing at the same moment. Miss Martineau says that, while in a mesmeric state, she saw "things out of other worlds—not the things themselves, but *impressions* of them." "They come," says she, "from my brain. The influence does not separate soul and body, but it sets the body at rest, while it exalts and elevates the thinking powers."

"A striking incident," says Miss M., "occurred in one of my earliest walks after recovery from a protracted illness. My mesmerist and I had reached a headland nearly half a mile from home, and were resting there, when she proposed to mesmerize me a little—partly to refresh me for our return, and partly to see if any effect would be produced in a new place, and while a fresh breeze was blowing. She merely laid her hand upon my forehead, and in a minute or two the usual appearances came, assuming a strange air of novelty from the scene in which I was. After the blurring of the outlines, which made all objects more dim than the dull gray day had already made them, the phosphoric lights appeared, glorifying every rock and headland, the horizon, and all the vessels in sight. One of the dirtiest and meanest of the steam tugs in the port was passing at the time, and it was all dressed in heavenly radiance—the last object that my imagination would select as an element of a vision. Then, and often before and since, did it occur to me, that if I had been a pious and very ignorant Catholic, I could not have escaped the persuasion that I had seen heavenly visions. Every glorified object before my eyes would have been a revelation; and my mesmerist, with the white halo around her head, and the illumined profile, would have been a saint or an angel."

We know not whether, in this instance, the mesmerist *willed* her subject to behold things as she did, yet as to the general truth *that the will of the operator can produce in the subject mesmerized those states of mind and body which he wills him or her to experience*, there is abundant evidence. O. S. Fowler, editor of the Phrenological Journal, says he "can bear ample testimony to the fact, as he has seen, experienced, and *induced* similar states by the thousand." And many others testify to the same effect.

Persons can be made to travel to other countries, and even to other spheres, and come back and tell what they have seen. And as persons vary in the talent of description and observation, in the normal state, so do they vary in a semi-abnormal condition. Some are found to be *better travellers*, and will see more than others, and in spiritual things will differ in their descriptions as they differ in religious creeds and sentiments. Thus a Swedenborg, or a Fishbough, sees a hell in the future state, where sinners suffer the penalty of their earthly sins; while an Ambler, or a Davis, discovers that all men are alike joyful and happy. Mr. Davis has seen fit to caution the public not to believe too quickly or too fully the things excitable persons relate; "because some minds are naturally inclined to exaggerate or enlarge upon every thing which they may feel, see, or hear." The *state* alluded to is merely *induced*. It is not real.

Persons are frequently made to do what they believe is done by others, as in the case of a son of Dr. Phelps, of Stratford, Connecticut. The boy, on one occasion, was found (with a rope passed under his arms) suspended to the limb of a tree, having been taken, as was supposed, from his bed in the evening by spirits, and thus treated by them. The boy declared that when it was done, he "screamed at the top of his voice;" but it was ascertained that he made no noise at all, for if he had, the domestics, who were in the kitchen when he passed through it, must have heard him, which they did not. We have the testimony of A. J. Davis, himself, that the boy "really supposed that he had called aloud; and so far from having been tied to the tree *by spirits, he had been made unconsciously instrumental in tying himself to the tree!*" "I have heard," says Mr. Davis, "instances of mischief cited, as occurring in Dr. Phelps's house, in evidence of *satanic agency*, which I now discover to have been caused or accomplished by one of the children in sport, sometimes by electrical discharges and magnetic attractions, and sometimes by the almost unpardonable mischievousness of persons unknown to the family. The wanton destruction of property alleged to have taken place on this gentleman's premises is referable, in most cases, to emanations of vital electricity, seeking its equilibrium in the atmosphere. In this manner window panes were broken and furniture injured. In Woodbridge, New York, some few years ago, a young lady was affected with a disease which gave rise to similar phenomena. Mysterious sounds were heard in her presence; window panes were frequently broken in her vicinity; and, in like manner, door panels were burst out, sometimes falling *towards* her, sometimes *from* her, and quick, concussive, and very loud sounds were heard under her feet as she ascended a flight of stairs. Ultimately, the mysterious phenomena frightened her into an illness which cured the malady."

"People cannot be too cautious how they receive the doings of those who profess to be in connection with spirits of the other spheres; and to those who wish to inquire into the matter, we would say, Go and hear, but try to keep your wits about you, and not swallow bodily either the preachers or their strange affirmations."—*Horace Greely*.

"Under an impression that whatever is communicated by a spirit must, of course, be true, many persons are receiving these communications as the truth of God—as a new revelation from the spirit world. But if these communications are from spirits, we have no proof that they are good spirits. The presumption is, that they are bad spirits—lying spirits. At my house they often accused each other of lying—contradicted at one time what they affirmed at another; inflicted injury upon property in the most wanton manner; and have given conclusive evidence throughout that the discipline of hell, which they profess to have experienced for several years, has not been wholly effectual in improving their characters, and qualifying them for the 'higher spheres' for which many suppose that the discipline after death is a preparation."—*Dr. Phelps*.

"Many of the doings of the rapping spirits are too nonsensical and absurd to be believed. They spoil all our notions of the dignity, the *spirituality*, of the spiritual world. That a messenger should come from the spirit land to tell an old woman that her black cat did eat another old woman's white rabbit, is not in accordance with the ideas most people have of the doings and missions of beings in the enjoyment of an immortal state."—*Puritan Recorder*.

PERSONS TRAINED BY A LECTURER.

We have been informed, by a certain mesmerizer, that a distinguished lecturer upon magnetism frequently trains persons to enact certain parts in his public exhibitions. He first puts them under mesmeric influence, and while in that state they are instructed to say certain things, or to perform certain acts, which he wishes to exhibit at some subsequent lecture. To this they severally agree, and thus a regular programme, or series of performances, is made out. They are then brought out of the mesmeric state, having been previously willed by the operator to forget all that has passed while in that state. At the next meeting appointed, these persons are present, and are again put into the same state as before, when they immediately perceive, and are ready to perform, the several parts assigned to them. In fact, they are so completely under the will and control of the lecturer, that they *must* do or say *what he wills them to do or say*, and they cannot help it, neither can they have the least recollection of what has transpired, after being restored to the normal state.

SCENE AT EAST BOSTON.

We were present at a "circle," at the house of a *medium* in East Boston, on the 30th of April, 1852. Instead of that decorum and seriousness that might be expected while holding intercourse with departed spirits, we were surprised at the levity and sport indulged on the occasion. The spirits were laughed at, and scolded, because they made so many blunders in spelling out names, and were urged and coaxed to do better. A lady, who had buried a friend, was told that the name of the deceased was *Hannah*. But she informed the medium that it was a *brother* she had buried, and that she had never lost a *sister*. But the medium said it made no difference, as the spirits often gave the name of a sister for a brother, and sometimes a cousin for either, as they were all in the family connection, and all such dwelt together in the Love Circles.

In spelling out the name of any deceased friend, you are presented with a card containing the alphabet, and are required to commence with the letter A, and go through the alphabet some one, two, or three times, touching each letter with a pencil as you pass over it. On touching some particular letter, a rap is given, indicating that it is the first letter of the name of your departed friend. And so of the other letters comprising the name. The spirits often made mistakes in rapping at the wrong letter, and were required to try again till they got the spelling right. We were very particular to observe that the spirit was sure to rap whenever the inquirer stopped or hesitated in passing over any letter. Five or six would be eagerly watching the movement of your hand, and the least possible hesitation upon any one letter was sure to be accompanied with simultaneous raps. And as the inquirer was frequently cautioned to proceed slow, it was natural enough to hesitate on those letters comprising the name as it was spelled in their own mind. In this way the alphabet became an interpreter to the supposed spirits.

We requested that some demonstrations should be given in the art of table lifting, but were told that the gentleman through whose agency the feat is performed was not present this evening. We inquired if it was necessary that any particular gentleman should be present that tables or chairs might be raised, and were told it was, and that the gentleman in question seemed to carry a large amount of electricity in a circle about his person.

We have been informed by another person, who says he has, and often does, raise tables and other articles, by request of others, that he does it by controlling the vital electricity of individuals present at the time. He says he "*steals*" their vital electricity, and appropriates it to his own use, although those from whom he thus takes it are not conscious of the fact. The more persons there are in the room, the larger the amount of electricity obtained, and the greater the effects produced by it. There is nothing as yet performed by those alleged to be in connection with spirits but what he can successfully imitate, such as producing effects upon persons at a distance, imitating the handwriting of absent or deceased persons unknown to him causing persons to write music, poetry, &c., who, in a normal state, are incapable of doing either, as well as many other exploits, at the option or desire of those who are present; inquirers, oftentimes, in such cases, becoming the operators, transferring their own impressions, ideas, sentiments, and knowledge to the acting medium, and yet entirely ignorant of the fact, and astonished at the results produced. The gentleman referred to discards the agency of spirits in these transactions, and declares that the whole is done by the power of his own will in using and controlling the amount of electricity present at the time; thus proving that the mind or spirit in the body has as much power and control over electricity as the mind or spirit has *out* of, or separate from, the body. And he is of the opinion that if scientific men would investigate the powers of electricity, and the laws by which it is controlled, they would no more think of attributing the phenomena of the times to the agency of *spirits*, than to the Pope of Rome. Many engaged in producing these phenomena are themselves ignorant of the power or means by which they are produced, and therefore attribute them to *spiritual* agency, which is, in fact, transferring the whole matter to a point beyond human investigation, where no mortal being can possibly explore.

Some seem to think that these modern developments must be the work of spirits, because, amid all the opposition arraigned against them, they still continue to progress, and are becoming more and more wonderful every day. Yet the same argument is as conclusive and convincing in favor of Mormonism, and other foolish and wicked extravagances, as it is in favor of the alleged spiritual manifestations. But while hundreds, and perhaps thousands, are marvelling at the strangeness of these developments, we find that several who have been engaged in them for months or years, and believed them to be emanations from the spirit world, now declare their convictions to the contrary, as will be seen by the following account from the pen of a distinguished writer, Professor Pond, of Maine.

EXTRACT FROM THE PURITAN RECORDER.

"The feats of the ancient jugglers were many of them mere acts of deception. They were known to be such by those who performed them. And the same is true of many who practise the like things now. Their rappings and writings, and other strange performances, are secretly, artfully got up by themselves. I do not say that this is true in all cases; but in some cases we *know* it is true; because the matter has been fully investigated, and public confession has been made. For example: A young woman, who had been instructed by the Rochester rappers, and practised the art with them for a time, afterwards renounced it, and exposed the delusion to the world. 'All who saw her and heard her,' says my informant, 'were entirely satisfied of the truth of her statements, and that she had revealed the actual method in which the deception was effected and the deluded were blinded. Another young woman in Providence, Almira Beazely, who was noted for her rappings and revelations, and who murdered her brother to accomplish one of her own predictions, confessed, on her trial, that she made the noises herself, and explained the manner in which they were produced. She also confessed to the removal of certain articles in the house which had strangely disappeared, and which she pretended had been *taken away by spirits*. Drs. Lee and Flint, of Buffalo, assisted by two gentlemen by the name of Burr, have very thoroughly investigated the matter, and explained the manner in which the mysterious noises are made. Mr. Burr has himself made the rappings, and made them so loud as to be heard by a congregation of fifteen hundred people.

"These instances are sufficient to prove that the spiritual manifestations of our times, like those of ancient times, are in many instances a sheer deception—a vile trick, palmed off upon a wondering and credulous community, for the sake of money, or for other sinister and selfish ends. If there is any thing more than trick in these spiritual manifestations,—and I am inclined to think that, in some instances, there may be,—I should refer it, as in case of the ancient wizards, to the influence of *occult natural causes*— perhaps electricity, or animal magnetism, or something else, operating upon a nervous system of peculiar sensibility. I incline to this opinion for several reasons.

"In the first place, if the noises and other manifestations were really the work of spirits, why should they not be made through one person, as well as another? Why should not all mediums be alike? Whereas it is confessed that only persons of a peculiar nervous temperament are capable of becoming mediums.

"Again: if the disclosures which are made are really from the spirit world, it might be expected that they would, at least, be *consistent with themselves*. Whereas it is well known that they vary endlessly. In numerous instances, they are directly self-contradictory. 'Some of the communications,' says one who had been a medium, 'were orthodox; others were infidel. Some would acknowledge the truth of the Bible; others would condemn it. Some would be in favor of virtue; others would encourage the grossest crimes.'

"Another man, who had been a noted medium, but who was beginning to get his eyes opened as to the character of the proceedings, told his audience one night, 'Now, any one present ask a series of questions, and I pledge myself that the answer shall be, every time, yes.' Some one in the company asked, 'Is John Thompson alive?' The answer was, 'Yes.' 'Is John Thompson dead?' 'Yes.' 'Does John Thompson live in Vermont?' 'Yes.' 'Does he live in Massachusetts?' 'Yes.' And so the spirits went on contradicting themselves times without number. After this, a like series of questions were answered in the negative, exhibiting the most glaring contradictions, just as the operator pleased.

"But this brings me to another reason for supposing that the answers are not from departed spirits, but rather from the *mind of the operator*, or from *some other mind in communication with his*, under the influence of an electric or magnetic cause. It is an admitted fact that these answers coincide very generally with the opinions or wishes of the medium, or of some one present in consultation with him. I knew a very respectable man, who discovered that he was a medium, and who practised various experiments upon himself. Upon being asked what he thought of it, he replied, 'If the answers are from the spirits, they must be *very silly spirits*; for they always answer just as I wish to have them.' Another medium informs us that he can obtain any answer he pleases, by fixing his mind strongly upon it at the time. Now, does this look as though the answer came from spirits? If the spirits of the dead spoke, they would be likely to speak out independently; to speak just what *they* thought, and not what those thought with whom they were consulting.

"There is another circumstance to be noted in this connection. When the requisite preparation is made, there is no need of consulting the spirits at all, in order to secure answers. You may consult with the chairs or the table just as well. This experiment was tried, not long since, at Wilmington, Vermont. A Mr. Kellogg was the medium, and he had succeeded in consulting the spirits to the satisfaction of all concerned. At length he remarked that he was about to let the company into an important secret. 'We will interrogate the *table*,' said he, 'and have nothing more to do with spirits.' He did so; and the *table talked and answered, just as the spirits had done before*. At the same time the table was made to stand on one leg, and to move about, as is usual in such cases. This experiment demonstrated, to the satisfaction of all present, that the strange appearances could be produced just as well without the spirits as with them. 'The calling for spirits,' to use the language of my informant, 'is mere garnish and fog, by which the real agency in the case is concealed.'

"On the point now under consideration, viz., the possibly *electric* character of these manifestations, I am happy to introduce the testimony of Dr. Samuel Taylor, a respectable physician of Petersham, Massachusetts, whose article on the subject may be found in a late number of the Boston Medical and Surgical Journal. Dr. Taylor discovered accidentally that he was a medium, and he proceeded to make experiments upon himself. The manifestation, in his case, was not by rapping, but by writing—a much more convenient mode of communicating with the spirit world. On taking his pen, and holding himself in a peculiar attitude, and proposing mentally some question to the spirits, his pen would begin to oscillate in his fingers, and very soon would write out an answer; and this without any voluntary effort of his own. And what is particularly to be noticed is, the pen would always write an answer which accorded with his own opinion or wishes, that is, if he had any wish on the subject. For example: Dr. Taylor inquired of one of the spirits about the different forms of religion. 'I asked which was the best religion, at the same time fixing my mind sternly on the word *Protestant*. My hand immediately wrote *Protestant*. In the same manner, and *by direction of the same spirit*, my hand wrote successively, *Methodist*, *Unitarian*, and I believe one or two others. While in this state,' Dr. Taylor says, '*I felt a sensation like that of a light galvanic current passing through me*. Sometimes it appeared to be a steady thrill, and sometimes it was intermittent, resembling light shocks of electricity.'

"After numerous experiments, Dr. Taylor comes to the conclusion, that the strange phenomena of which he was the subject were not tricks of his own, neither did they come from the spirit world, but were the result of what he calls *detached vitalized electricity*. When this conclusion had been formed in his own mind, it occurred to him that he would put it to the test of the spirits themselves. 'Accordingly I asked them,' says he, 'if this was the work of departed spirits. The answer was, "No." I asked if it was the work of the devil. Again the answer was, "No." I asked if it was the effect of *detached vitalized electricity*. The answer was, "Yes."' So the spirits *confirmed* the conclusion to which the doctor had come, as they did, in fact, all his conclusions.

"We have the testimony of another medium, of the same import with that of Dr. Taylor. Mr. Benjamin F. Cooley, who had long been a believer and operator in the spiritual rappings, states that his mind is now entirely changed. This change was brought about in consequence of 'a deep and earnest study of the nature, power, and application of electricity, and of the susceptibility of the mind to electrical or psychological changes.' These things, he says, will produce the same mysterious and startling phenomena which have been produced throughout the country, and attributed to the operations of departed spirits. (Mr. Cooley has recently published a work entitled An Exposition of Spiritual Manifestations, to which we would refer the reader.)

"A part of what is done by those who claim to have familiar spirits, may be the result of unknown *natural causes*. This is the most plausible and excusable view which can possibly be taken of these practices; and yet, even in this view, they are frightfully evil. The persons who alone are susceptible to the influence of these natural causes are generally those of a diseased or delicate nervous temperament; and the effect of experimenting upon their nervous system is usually to shatter it the more. They become excitable, fantastic, and often insane. Diseases are engendered, both of body and mind, which lead on to the most fearful consequences. But a short time ago, the papers gave an account of a man in Barre, Massachusetts, who had been much given to the rappings and other spiritual manifestations, who became, in consequence, a raving maniac, threatening the life of his family, and was committed to the Lunatic Asylum at Worcester. Other like instances are occurring frequently, from the same cause. Almira Beazely, the Providence rapper, who murdered her brother in fulfilment of one of her own predictions, was cleared on the ground of her insanity.

"But this is not the only evil of the practices in question, when viewed as the result of natural causes. For the truth is, that, in most cases, they are *not so viewed* by those who engage in them. *They* regard them as the work of spirits. They are, therefore, deceived; and those who follow them are deceived. Both suppose they are receiving utterances from the other world, when nothing is uttered but vain fantasies from their own minds and hearts. Such a deception is, manifestly, a hurtful one. It is full of danger to all concerned. To mistake one's own fancies for divine revelation, and feel conscience-bound to obey them as such, is the very essence of *fanaticism*. It is fanaticism in its most frightful form. Under the influence of such an impression, persons may be led to perpetrate the greatest cruelties, and the most horrid crimes, and vainly think that they are doing God service. The wretched man in Barre was led to attempt the life of his family, in obedience to a supposed revelation from the spirit world.

"The practices which have been considered are of heathen origin. They originated with the ancient heathen; they were spread over a greater part of the heathen world; and they continue to pervade and curse it to the present time. Among numerous heathen tribes at the present day, scarcely a calamity occurs—a death, a flood, a fit of sickness, or an instance of death—but some poor creature (and often more than one) is accused and put to death, as being the cause of it. 'The sick man is bewitched: who has bewitched him? His death (if he chance to die) has been brought about by evil spirits: who has sent the spirits upon him?' To get an answer to these questions, some old hag or conjurer is consulted; the cause of the mischief is quickly discovered, and an innocent person is put to death. Probably hundreds die every year after this manner, among the heathen, *even in this nineteenth century*! And the case would soon be no better among ourselves, if we were to go, extensively and *confidently*, into the practice of consulting with familiar spirits. The spirits would unravel all mysteries for us; they would reveal all secrets; and not a man, woman, or child would long be safe from their malicious accusations.

"Something more than a year ago, the Lunatic Asylum in Maine took fire, and a portion of its inmates were smothered and consumed. And there are hundreds of persons now in the state, who affirm that the building was set on fire by the keepers, with a view to cover up and conceal their own wickedness. These persons *know* it was so; they have not the shadow of a doubt on the subject. Why? Not that they have a particle of evidence to this effect from our world, but because the spirits have so informed them. Now, let these utterances become common, and be commonly received, and in three months' time those keepers might every one of them be dragged to the gallows, or the stake, while they were as innocent of the charge laid against them as a child unborn.

"I refer to this instance just to show the sin, the evil, the exceeding peril, of indulging in those practices which have been exposed. Let all those who read these things, then, beware of them and shun them. If any of us are capable of becoming *mediums*, as they are called, we had better not know it; or, if we know it, we had better refrain from all experiments. To tamper with such a power is to tamper with an already shattered nervous system, the only effect of which will be to shatter it the more.

"There is nothing more striking than the difference between those representations of the future world which are made known in the Bible, and which we know are true, and those which are put forth by the revealers of our own times. The former are solemn, exciting, impressive, some of them awfully so, others gloriously. While the latter, as Professor Stowe says, are 'so uniformly and monotonously silly, that we are compelled to think, if these are really the spirits of the dead, in dying they must have lost what little of common sense they ever possessed. If these are actual specimens of the spiritual world, then this world, hard and imperfect as it is, is altogether the most respectable part of God's creation.'

"In the Bible, we have frequent accounts of persons who were raised from the dead—who actually returned from the spirit world to this. But they returned uniformly with sealed lips. In not a single instance did they make any disclosures. But our modern revealers pursue a very different course. They practise no reserve. They go into the minutest particulars,—sometimes into the most disgusting details,—and publish, as one expresses it, 'a penny magazine of the spiritual world.'"

In the language of the Puritan Recorder, "The worst of the evil is the soul-hardening familiarity they produce with the most awful subjects ever offered for human contemplation. We know of nothing in human experience so fatally destructive of all that reverence for the spiritual, that awe of the unseen, that tender emotion, as well as solemn interest, which connect themselves with the idea of the other life. Who, that has a Christian heart, would not prefer the silence of the grave to the thought of the dear departed one in the midst of such imaginings, and such scenic associations as are usually connected with the performances of the spirit rappers? 'They are not dead, but *sleep.*' 'They enter into *peace,*' says the prophet. And then the precious and consoling addition—'They sleep in Jesus;' meaning, beyond all doubt, a state of rest, of calmness, of security, of undisturbed and beatific vision—far removed from all resemblance to this bustling life—a state in all respects the opposite of that which fancy pictures as belonging to the scenes presented in the manifestations of spiritual rappings, and spiritual table liftings and all those spiritual pantomimes, which seem to be becoming more and more extravagant and grotesque in proportion to the infidel credulity with which they are received."

Should any think, by reading what we have offered upon this subject in the preceding pages, that we have imputed guilt and deception to mediums, who are believed to be, many of them, above such trickery, we would merely refer such to page 29 of the Reply of Veriphilos Credens to the communications supposed to have been written by Dr. Enoch Pond, professor in the Bangor Seminary, as published in the columns of the Puritan Recorder. The reviewer says, "To suppose that mediums could practise deception on men of shrewdness and caution implies a greater credulity than does a faith in the most startling of their performances." "There is not the slightest degree of evidence," says this writer, "that such a case has ever occurred;" and yet on the selfsame page he says, "*There is no doubt that some mediums, when the sounds and motions have failed to come in the usual mysterious way, have counterfeited them by some sly motions of their feet and hands. I have seen such things done, in some instances!*"

The same author says, page 63, "I have not attempted to justify any reliance on disclosures made to us in the way of rappings. I think it *altogether* unsafe to do so, for the declaration has already come to us, from what purports to be the spirits themselves, that *all these manifestations are of a low order*, and are produced by the *lowest grade of spirits*."

As to the plea that "spirits *must* make the sounds," to account for the *intelligence* communicated, it being impossible for mere "*electricity* to originate facts," we reply by affirming that there is no intelligence given beyond a certain limit; i.e., the mind of some one or ones in connection, either present or absent, for it makes no difference. For available purposes, a person a thousand or ten thousand miles distant may yield all the amount of intelligence required in a given case. Distance is no obstacle whatever. Electricity counts neither time nor space. For instance, the transmission of electricity through a conducting substance is instantaneous. A wire, or other conductor, may have motion communicated to its whole length at the same moment, whatever that length may be; and it is stated that an electro-magnetic impulse may be transmitted at the rate of one hundred and eighty thousand miles in a second, thus outstripping the sun in its march!

A large number of intelligent individuals, who, for a year or two past, have instituted a series of experiments upon this matter of "intelligence," have found that in no case has information been imparted beyond what existed in their own minds or that of some kindred or friend. Finding this to be the case, they have wisely come to the conclusion that spirits have never originated a solitary idea; that is, *disembodied spirits*; and as to the spirit within a man, in his corporeal state, why cannot it command as much influence over vital electricity as in its disembodied existence? Since both parties claim to perform by the same agent, and both claim this agent to be that of *vital electricity*, we have also come to the same conclusion, with a host of others, that the "calling for spirits is mere garnish and fog, by which the real agency in the case is concealed."

EXTRACT FROM THE HOME JOURNAL.

"A considerable heap of books, pamphlets, and periodicals, some against, but most of them for, the 'spiritual phenomena,' has been accumulating upon our table, and now looms up large before us, demanding notice. That departed spirits have any thing to do with them is an explanation that we have never been able to accept for one moment. We should as soon think of asserting that an apple, rolling suddenly at our feet, must necessarily have fallen out of heaven, because we could not see the tree it had blown from. To bring such an astounding theory to explain such trivial phenomena is like sending a frigate to pick up a champagne bottle that might be floating down the bay.

"By some of the works before us we are informed, among many other things, that in the other world every man has his name upon his front door; that Swedenborg is a great man, delivers lectures, and *has a street named after him*; that in heaven parties, concerts, and *converzationes* are frequent; that at some of the concerts, star singers of great celebrity perform, attracting inconceivable multitudes of spirits to hear them; that children take lessons in French and Italian every morning; that the space allotted to some of the spirits is as large as New York; that the 'seventh sphere' (the highest heaven) is about five thousand miles from the earth; that the beds are of roses, and when the spirits recline upon them, the birds sing joyfully around, and mingle their music with the perfume of the flowers; that the celestials (not the Chinese) wear white robes, edged with pink; that a man generally attends his own funeral; that spirits, on their arrival in heaven, are set to studying geology, chemistry, and other dull subjects, which they soon begin to like, and say their daily lessons with an excellent grace; that parchment is in extensive use; that spirits are allowed to visit 'earth' once a day only, and have the privilege of staying one hour; that they have books, rings, newspapers, robin redbreasts, fruit, lakes, streams, diamonds, and drawing masters in the next world. 'Dora's dress,' says one of the revelations, 'was of blue satin, with a white sash; half sleeves, full; a pink velvet ribbon round her throat, fastened by a cameo. Her hair was in curls each side of her face, and fastened in a knot behind.' Dora, be it observed, is a departed *spirit*.

"If it could be shown that all these things were really revealed, as they are said to be, we should still think them unworthy of notice. The greater part of the 'supernal theology' is utterly frivolous; and whether frivolous or not, it bears very plainly the impress of the medium's own mind, or of the unknown desires of those by whom he is surrounded. If we were called upon to minister to a mind diseased, or to find pabulum for a soul hungering after moral excellence, we should as soon think of offering a copy of the Arabian Nights' Entertainments as a book of the 'supernal theology.' For the practical guidance of life, there is more help in any two maxims of the Sermon on the Mount, than in the whole literature of supernaturalism.

"The manifestation mania would have died away long since but for one unfortunate circumstance. We have in our land a large number of men who may be termed semi-clergymen, or, as they are frequently called, 'outsiders,' or 'come-outers.' These are they who, either because they know too much or because they know too little, or from superfluity of naughtiness or redundancy of virtue, find it difficult to obtain a 'settlement.' These are the men who foster delusions; who, because they cannot find a way to *serve* the public, are reduced to *prey* upon it. They embrace the new light—whatever it may be—with a degree of sincerity, and commit themselves to it; then they push it, stimulate it, make a business of it, and live by it. O the multitude of spiritual delusions that in every age of the world have originated and derived their strength solely from the fact that the bodily necessities of certain individuals depended upon their perpetuity! That, at this moment, there are men most diligently engaged in the new spiritual line, for the purpose of securing by it a reprieve from starvation, (or work,) is a fact which we do not merely believe, but *know*."

FORETELLING FUTURE EVENTS.

Many devices have been resorted to in order to foretell the events of the future. Some pretend to do it by cards; some by the settlings of a tea or coffee cup; some by astrology; some by tables of letters and figures; some by the lines of the hand; and some by spirits of the dead. Strenuous advocates of these various modes are found, who recount the wonderful predictions that have taken place. Some spirit hunter recently prognosticated that the ship Staffordshire (reported to be lost) would arrive safe at San Francisco on a certain day, as she did. Professor Anderson had a glass bell at the Melodeon, in Boston, in September, 1852, that answered questions pertaining to future events. In deciding upon who would be the next president, it gave six distinct taps for Pierce—the number agreed upon if he was to be the successful competitor. This was done without any aid from spirits. We very much doubt whether Robach or Lester would refuse a challenge from A. J. Davis himself, to test their respective claims to correct predictions. Yet we do not believe that any reliance can be placed upon the prophecies of either party. Events may sometimes transpire in accordance with their predictions; and it would be strange if they did not, as they are always predicting, and events are ever occurring. But they never think of naming the multiplicity of failures that take place. Not long since, the spirits said that a distant friend would never live to reach home; but he soon after arrived, safe and well. Mr. Lester told a young man of Woburn that in two years he would marry a certain young lady; but in two months he was a corpse. Hundreds of such failures are constantly occurring, but are kept out of sight. If generally known, they would spoil the trade. We are surprised that men professing to high attainments, as A. J. Davis and some of his coadjutors, should fall back and plant themselves upon such stale trash. Some two years since, while lying apparently near our end, a lady suggested to us that, if we desired, she would consult Mr. Lester upon the probability of our recovery. We declined the offer, choosing to leave all with the Sovereign Disposer of events, believing that he would permit nothing to take place but what would be for our best good, and that of all concerned.

"Heaven from all creatures hides the book of fate,

All but the page prescribed—their *present state*;

From brutes what men, from men what angels know;

Or who could suffer being here below?

The lamb thy riot dooms to bleed to-day,

Had he thy reason, would he skip and play?

Pleased to the last, he crops the flowery food,

And licks the hand just raised to shed his blood.

O, blindness to the future! kindly given,

That each may fill the circle marked by Heaven.

Hope humbly then, with trembling pinions soar;

Wait the great teacher death, and God adore!

What future bliss he gives not thee to know,

But gives *that hope* to be thy *blessing now*."—POPE.

VISIONS, MIRACLES, AND WONDERS.

The writings of the spirit rappers abound with accounts of sights, sounds, visions, and wonders. We are forcibly reminded of a similar display in the writings of the Adventists, previous to the predicted end of the world in 1843—an overwhelming array of facts, calculations, signs, visions, wonders, miracles, maps, pictures, drawings, and hieroglyphics, all going to show, in the most positive manner, that in that year the world would be annihilated. And still it remains; and the works containing the omens and facts to substantiate the prediction are called to share the fate of a Farmer's Almanac quite out of date. Some few still hold on to a semblance of the theory, like him who, in the spring of 1851, declared that a talking cow, somewhere in Maine, had prophesied that the world would be burned up the following June. How lamentable to view the numbers of men and women who have given heed to such things, when assured that the day and the hour is not known even by the Son himself. (Matt. xxiv. 36.) Many of these persons were once active in the church, and exerted an influence for good; but by remaining in their present position, their influence in the cause of Christ is palsied, and their, talents buried in the earth. And yet we have propounded to us another "NEW CHURCH," which, according to the predictions of its adherents, is destined to destroy all other churches, as it *was to be*, according to the predictions of Miller, Fitch, Himes, and others.

In conclusion upon these things, we would add, that it has been our belief from the first, that there is nothing supernatural in the so-called *spiritual manifestations*. They all bear the marks of *earthly* origin. The public not knowing how to explain them, the first rappings were attributed to the "spirits;" and the idea having been set afloat, it has been adopted without investigation, being the easiest way of accounting for it.

To the common mind, three hundred years ago, it was plain and easy, that the world was *flat*, and rested on something—on the *back of Atlas*, and he stood on a *tortoise*, and the tortoise again on *something*; and the fact that nobody could tell what, was not allowed to stumble any one; it rested on a *foundation*, and that was enough for any one to know or believe. Motion, space, attraction, and repulsion were not understood, and Galileo came near losing his life, and did lose his personal liberty and character, for intelligence. When the world is as fully instructed in certain principles connected with our existence as it is in the laws of the physical universe, the "rappings," we think, will cease to be a wonder.

CLAIRVOYANT PHYSICIANS.

Persons in a clairvoyant state, by being put in connection with a diseased person, feel, by sympathy, the pain and disease of the patient. But to be qualified to describe the locality of the disease, or be able to tell what organ or part is affected, the practitioner must first have studied anatomy and physiology. The more perfect they are in these branches, the more accurately can they describe the seat of the disease. Their remedies are mostly botanical, and are generally safe in their operation. The *regular* "clairvoyant physician," so to speak, does not pretend to be in league with "spirits;" but there *are* those who profess that their prescriptions come from the other world—from those who, though dead, rest *not* from their labors. Notwithstanding the extreme simplicity of their remedies, such as any common nurse would advise, yet such is the profound sanctity and mystery thrown around them by an *unseen spirit*, that some profess to have received "wonderful healing mercies." To *believe* that a medicine (however simple) is prescribed by a *spirit* from above, is enough to perform a cure in any case. Imagination alone is equal to the task. A very eminent allopathic physician informs us that he often rolls up brown bread pills, which, in certain cases, perform unmistakable cures. In fact, history is full of recoveries wrought out by aid of the imagination. We will subjoin a case by way of illustration.

"Sir Humphrey Davy, on one occasion in early life, was assisting Dr. Beddoes in his experiments on the inhalation of nitrous oxide. Dr. Beddoes having inferred that this agent must be a specific for palsy, a patient was selected for trial, and placed under the care of Davy. Previously to administering the gas, Davy inserted a small thermometer under the tongue of the patient, to ascertain the temperature. The paralytic man, wholly ignorant of the process to which he was to submit, but deeply impressed by Dr. Beddoes with the certainty of its success, no sooner felt the thermometer between his teeth, than he concluded the talisman was in operation, and in a burst of enthusiasm declared that he had already experienced the effects of its benign influence throughout his whole body. The opportunity was too tempting to be lost. Davy did nothing more, but desired his patient to return on the following day. The same ceremony was repeated, the same result followed; and at *the end of a fortnight he was dismissed wholly cured*; no remedy of any kind, except the thermometer, having ever been used."

STYLE OF "SUPERNAL" COMPOSITIONS.

In the "supernal" productions we are presented with a pedantic display of high-sounding words and phrases. To use the language of inspiration, "they speak great swelling words of vanity." A work has recently been announced with this imposing title: "MACROCOSM and MICROCOSM," containing, among other things, "*The Potential Media*," "*The Diastole and Systole of Nature*." A writer in the Spiritual Telegraph, of October 9, says, "There are very many fancy-captivating, and depravity-flattering publications—some of them filled with indications, the most specious and subtle, of a refined *atheism*. And I have seen a copy or two of a certain 'Journal,' ostensibly advocating the great truths (?) of spiritual manifestations, but containing some articles in which there was a congregation of words *superlatively unmeaning and transcendentally ridiculous*." The same writer says, "I do not believe one half the communications which are said to come from George Washington, Benjamin Franklin, Henry Clay, John C. Calhoun, John Wesley, and a host of other great names. What affinity can these spirits have with many of the thoughtless, light, and trifling circles, formed to pass off an hour, and perhaps ending with foolish mountebank scenes of psychology, falsely so called?"

Davis, in his Great Harmonia, page 206, exposes a class of "mercenary practitioners, who claim extraordinary or supernatural powers for their subjects, *who give public and vulgar exhibitions, who employ chicanery and ignorant plans, who trifle with and play fantastic tricks with their subjects*." He speaks of a class of "doctrinal practitioners, who prevert and misinterpret principles and results; who labor to make the phenomena subservient to, and illustrative of, the theological dogmas; who receive, modify, or reject, as a sectarian education and prejudice may sanction; who conceal, misstate, and magnify disclosures." Enough, in all conscience, to condemn the whole farce.

MYSTERIOUS PHENOMENA, WITH THEIR AGENTS OR CAUSES.

A work has recently been issued in Boston, by E. C. Rogers, containing an exposition of mysterious agents, and dynamic laws, or science of moving powers. It is a very valuable work, and, with his consent, we shall take the liberty of introducing some of the principal facts adduced; and at the same time would advise every inquirer to purchase the work for himself, which he will never have cause to regret.

On page 22, the author says, "Light and heat have always been known as agents by the common sensation of their more palpable phenomena. But electricity and magnetism were not known until their phenomena were specially observed. Many of the facts of these agents, before the latter had become known, were referred to spiritual agencies. It is the tendency of ignorance, in every age, to do the same thing. Reason demands an agent adequate to the production of every phenomenon. If she has not been furnished with sufficient data by which to arrive at a correct conclusion, imagination, influenced by a blind marvellousness, will refer the phenomena to some supernatural cause. Hence the early superstitions about chemical operations, the appearance of comets, eclipses, meteors, the 'bog lights,' and a thousand other phenomena. But as the agencies of nature have become known, and their laws and conditions of action discovered, the domination of superstition has given place to the triumph of reason and the reign of truth."

"Reason determines that, for every phenomenon, there is an agent; but never, without sufficient data, does she determine what that agent is. The imagination often assumes this prerogative, and gives conclusions without *facts*, or furnishes the false data from which the logical faculty draws false principles. We mention these things to show how easy it is to be deceived, by our imaginations, with regard to the causes of outward phenomena, and that the only legitimate and trustworthy process in arriving at a solution of the mysteries of nature is, to furnish the reason with *facts*, and exclude the influence of imagination. A blind precipitation of faith is also a fatal influence to all correct reasoning; for it rouses the action of the imagination, and long before the reason can possibly give a correct deduction, credulity and imagination have conjured one up; and this will be the more insisted upon as the only correct conclusion, as it is the least possessed of the real truth and the action of reason. Hence it is that those persons who are most ignorant of the principles of nature are the more positive and precipitate in their decisions upon any question of mystery.

They *know* that there is no natural explanation, and the man is a fool who *attempts* to find one." (Page 34.)

The first case we shall quote from the above work occurred in Woodbridge, New Jersey, and was published at the time in the Newark Daily Advertiser. The phenomena made their appearance in the family of Mr. J. Barron, consisting, for the most part, of unusual sounds accompanying a servant girl.

"The first sounds were those of a *loud thumping*, apparently against the side of the house, which commenced one evening, when the family had retired, and continued at short intervals until daylight, when it ceased.

"The next evening it commenced at nightfall, when it was ascertained to be mysteriously connected with the movements of a servant girl in the family—a white girl, about fourteen years of age. While passing a window, on the stairs, for example, a *sudden jar*, accompanied with an *explosive sound*, *broke a pane of glass*, the girl at the same time being seized with a violent spasm. This, of course, very much alarmed her; and the physician, Dr. Drake, was sent for, who came and bled her. The bleeding, however, produced no apparent effect. The noise still continued, as before, at intervals, wherever the girl went, each sound producing more or less of a spasm; and the physician, with all the family, remained up during the night. At daylight the *thumping* ceased again. In the evening the same thing was repeated, commencing a little earlier than before; and so every evening since, continuing each night until morning, and commencing each night a little earlier than before, until yesterday, when the thumping began about twelve o'clock at noon. The circumstances were soon generally spread through the neighborhood, and produced so much excitement that the house was filled, and surrounded from sunrise to sunset, for nearly a week. Every imaginable means were resorted to, in order to unravel the phenomenon. At one time the girl would be removed from one apartment to another, but without effect. Wherever she was placed, at certain intervals, the thumping would be heard in the room. She was taken to a neighboring house. The same result followed. When carried out of doors, however, no noise was heard. Dr. Drake, who was constant in his attendance during the whole period, occasionally aided by other scientific observers, was with us last evening for two hours, when we were politely allowed a variety of experiments with the girl, in addition to those heretofore tried, to satisfy ourselves that there is no imposition in the case, and, if possible, to discover the secret agent of the mystery. The girl was in an upper room, with a part of the family, when we reached the house. The noise then resembled that which would be produced by a person violently thumping the upper floor with the head of an axe, five or six times in succession, jarring the house, ceasing a few minutes, and then resuming as before. We were soon introduced into the apartment, and permitted to observe for ourselves. The girl appeared to be in perfect health, cheerful, and free from the spasms felt at first, and entirely relieved from every thing like the fear or apprehension which she manifested for some days. The invisible noise, however, continued to occur as before, though somewhat diminished in frequency, while we were in the room. In order to ascertain more satisfactorily that she did not produce it voluntarily, among other experiments we placed her on a chair on a blanket in the centre of the room, bandaged the chair with a cloth, fastening her feet on the front round, and confining her hands together on her lap. No change, however, was produced. The thumping continued as before, excepting that it was not quite so loud. The noise resembled that which would be produced by stamping on the floor with a heavy heel; yet she did not move a limb or muscle, that we could discover. She remained in this position long enough to satisfy all in the room that the girl exercised, voluntarily, no sort of agency in producing the noise. It was observed that the noise became greater the farther she was removed from any other person. We placed her in the doorway of a closet in the room, the door being ajar, to allow her to stand in the passage. In less than one minute the door flew open, as if violently struck with a mallet, accompanied with precisely such a noise as such a thump would produce. This was repeated several times, with the same effect. In short, in whatever position she was placed, whether in or out of the room, similar results, varied a little perhaps by circumstances, were produced. There is certainly no deception in the case. The noise was heard at least one hundred yards from the house."

"In this case, no suspicions were entertained by the investigators that there was any supernatural or spiritual power manifested, as there was no manifestations of intelligence. They were purely physical phenomena."

The next case we shall notice we copy from the Spiritual Telegraph of July 3, 1852, taken from an old New York paper, dated March 10, 1789. The extract is as follows:—

"Sir: Were I to relate the many extraordinary, though not less true accounts I have heard concerning that unfortunate girl at New Hackensack, your belief might perhaps be staggered and patience tired. I shall therefore only inform you of what I have been an eye-witness to. Last Sunday afternoon my wife and myself went to Dr. Thorn's, and after sitting for some time, we heard a knocking under the feet of a young woman that lives in the family; I asked the doctor what occasioned the noise: he could not tell, but replied, that he, together with several others, had examined the house, but were unable to discover the cause. I then took a candle and went with the girl into the cellar: there the knocking also continued; but as we were ascending the stairs to return, I heard a *prodigious rapping* on each side, which alarmed me very much. I stood still some time, looking around with amazement, when I beheld some lumber, which lay at the head of the stairs, shake considerably. About eight or ten days after, we visited the girl again: the knocking was again heard, but much louder than before. Our curiosity induced us to pay the third visit, when the phenomena were still more alarming. *I then saw the chairs move; a large dining table was thrown against me, and a small stand, on which stood a candle, was tossed up and thrown into my wife's lap;* after which we left the house, much surprised at what we had seen."

"Catharine Crowe, in her Night Side of Nature, mentions several well-authenticated cases of this character, and other writers have noticed the same phenomena. A case is given on the 410th page of Miss Crowe's work—that of a young officer in the English army, who, wherever he went, whether in camp or at home, or among strangers, was liable to be tormented with these *noises at night.* Although they gave no particular marks of intelligence, yet they were regarded by his relatives with an abundance of superstition. They considered him "haunted."

"When these sounds commenced, he would sit up in bed, and express his anger in strong execrations. If a cage bird was in his room, it was certain to be found dead in the morning; or if he kept a dog in the apartment, it would make away from him as soon as released, and never come near him again."

"The phenomena in Dr. Phelps's case, already mentioned in this volume, consisted in the moving of articles of furniture in a manner that could not be accounted for. Knives, forks, spoons, nails, blocks of wood, &c., were thrown in different directions about the house, when there appeared no visible power by which the motion could have been produced. A writer in the New Haven Journal and Courier testifies, that while he was present, "the contents of the pantry were emptied into the kitchen, and bags of salt, tin ware, and heavy cooking utensils were thrown in a promiscuous heap upon the floor, with a loud and startling noise. Loaves of delicious cake were scattered about the house. The large knocker of the outside door would thunder its fearful tones through the loud-resounding hall, chairs would deliberately move across the room, heavy marble-top tables would poise themselves upon two legs, and then fall with their contents to the floor—no person being within six feet of them."

"On the 1st of October, 1850, Mrs. Phelps and her two children left home for Pennsylvania: with this the phenomena ceased. The doctor remained at his house five weeks after, without disturbance. It was ascertained that these and other manifestations were less frequent and feebler when but one of the children was in the house; and that they were more frequent in connection with the lad, (one of the above children,) eleven years of age.

These children had frequently been mesmerized into the trance state by their father; and one of them was subject to spontaneous trance, and at one time was found in the barn in a cataleptic state. Since the return of the doctor's family, in the spring of 1851, he has kept the two children separate, the boy being away, lest his presence would occasion a recurrence of the same phenomena. Simultaneous with the phenomena, the boy would frequently start while asleep in bed.

Analogous to the above are the wonderful occurrences which took place at Stockwell, England, in January, 1772, as related in the work entitled Night Side of Nature, page 370. We shall only give the most important particulars of the case, leaving the reader to consult the work itself."

"On Monday, January 6, 1772, about ten o'clock in the forenoon, as Mrs. Golding (the hostess) was in the parlor, she heard the china and glasses in the kitchen tumble down and break; her maid came to her, and told her the stone plates were falling from the shelf; Mrs. Golding went into the kitchen, and saw them broken. Presently after, a row of plates from the next shelf fell down likewise, while she was there, and nobody near them: this astonished her much, and while she was thinking about it, other things in different places began to tumble about, some of them breaking, attended with violent noises all over the house; a clock tumbled down, and the case broke." The destruction increased with the wonder and terror of Mrs. Golding. Wherever she went, accompanied by the servant girl, this dreadful waste of property followed.

Mrs. Golding, in her terror, fled to a neighbor's, where she immediately fainted. A surgeon was called, and she was bled. The blood, which had hardly congested, was seen all at once to spring out of the basin upon the floor, and presently after, the basin burst to pieces, and a bottle of rum, that stood by it, broke at the same time.

Mrs. Golding went to a second neighbor's, as the articles she had conveyed to the first were being destroyed. And while the maid remained at the first neighbor's, Mrs. Golding was not disturbed; but when putting up what few things remained unbroken of her mistress's in a back apartment, a jar of pickles, that stood upon a table, turned upside down, and other things were broken to pieces.

Meantime the disturbances had ceased at Mrs. Golding's house, and but little occurred at the neighbors', while Mrs. Golding and her servant remained apart. But as soon as they came into each other's company, the disturbance would begin again.

About five o'clock on Tuesday morning, Mrs. Golding went to the chamber of her niece, and desired her to get up, as the noises and destruction were so great she could continue in the house no longer: at this time, all the tables, chairs, drawers, &c., were tumbling about. In consequence of this resolution, Mrs. Golding and her maid went over the way to Richard Fowler's. The maid returned to Mrs. Pain's, to help this lady dress her children. At this time all was quiet. They then repaired to Fowler's, and then began the same scenes as had happened at the other places. It must be remarked that all was quiet here as well as elsewhere, till the maid returned.

When they reached Mr. Fowler's, he began to light a fire in his back room. When done, he put the candlestick upon the table in the fore room. This apartment Mrs. Golding and her maid had just passed through. This candlestick, and another with a tin lamp in it, that stood by it, were dashed together, and fell to the ground. A lantern, with which Mrs. Golding had been lighted across the road, sprang from a hook to the ground. A basket of coals tumbled over, and the coals rolled about the room.

Mrs. Golding and her servant now returned home, when similar scenes were repeated. Mr. Pain then desired Mrs. Golding to send her maid for his wife to come to them. When she was gone all was quiet. When she returned she was immediately discharged, and no disturbances happened afterwards."

"The account gives us the following particulars, namely: that the phenomena always depended upon the presence of the servant maid, and that they always occurred with the greatest energy when the mistress was in the company of the maid; also that, when the maid passed through a room alone, there would be little or no disturbance of its contents, but if she was soon after followed by Mrs. Golding, various articles would begin to play the most singular pranks. Very often one article would be attracted by another, or they would fly towards each other, and striking together, fall upon the floor as if both had been charged with some physical agent which made them act like opposite poles. Then, also, they would fly *from* one another, as by *repulsive* forces. Every thing which Mrs. Golding had touched seems to have been in some way affected, so that afterwards, on the approach of the maid, it would be broken to atoms, sometimes, even, without her touch. The blood of Mrs. Golding was highly susceptible under the same circumstances, and the bowl in which it was contained and the glass ware standing by it burst to pieces."

"In the year 1835, a suit was brought before the sheriff of Edinburgh, Scotland, for the recovery of damages suffered in a certain house owned by a Mr. Webster. Captain Molesworth was the defendant at the trial." (See Night Side of Nature, page 400.) The following facts were developed: Mr.

Molesworth had seriously damaged the house both as to substance and reputation.

First. By sundry holes which he cut in the walls, tearing up the floors, &c., to discover the cause of certain noises which tormented himself and family.

Second. By the bad name he had given the house, stating that it was haunted. Witnesses for the defendant were sheriff's officers, justices of the peace, and officers of the regiment quartered near; all of whom had been at the said house sundry times to aid Captain Molesworth detect the invisible cause of so much disturbance.

The disturbance consisted in certain noises, such as knockings, pounding, scratching sounds, rustlings in different parts of a particular room; sometimes, however, in other parts of the house. Certain boards of the floor would seem to be at times infected with the noises; then certain points in the walls, at which Mr. Molesworth would point his gun, or cut into with an axe, all to no purpose.

The bed on which a young girl, aged thirteen years, had been confined by disease, would very often be raised above the floor, as if a sudden force was applied beneath it, which would greatly alarm her and the whole family, and cause the greatest perplexity. The concussions which were often produced on the walls would cause them visibly to tremble. The force that produced these results was soon discovered to be in some strange way connected with this invalid, and wherever the young invalid was moved this force accompanied her."

"It is plainly exhibited, in the cases just given, that no characteristics of spiritual agency are exhibited, but those, on the contrary, of a mere physical power, associated with the organism of certain persons. "We have not," says Mr. Rogers, "the least possible evidence that any spirit, demoniacal or angelic, had any hand in performing the wild antics among crockery and furniture which we have seen performed in the accounts given. For it is admitted that a spiritual agent is an intelligent agent. Its characteristics are those of intelligence, as every one admits. Wherever, therefore, these characteristics are wanting in a class of phenomena, it is blindly absurd, greatly superstitious, even to draw the inference that they are spiritual phenomena. But what shall be said when it is asserted as a veritable certainty, and the crowd is made to stretch their throats and swallow the absurdity without a moment's examination?" "Is it possible we are to be driven to the conclusion that the ground of faith in spirituality is identical with that of ignorance, superstition, fanaticism, bigotry?"

We shall now proceed to give the case of Angelique Cottin, as reported in the Night Side of Nature, and in the *Courrier des Etats Unis*, and the investigations of the case as reported by M. Arago, before the Paris Academy of Sciences, 16th of February, 1846.

"Angelique Cottin was a native of La Perriere, aged fourteen, when, on the 15th of January, 1846, at eight o'clock in the evening, while weaving silk gloves at an oaken frame, in company with other girls, the frame began to jerk, and they could not by any efforts keep it steady. It seemed as if it were alive; and becoming alarmed, they called in the neighbors, who would not believe them, but desired them to sit down and go on with their work. Being timid, they went one by one, and the frame remained still till Angelique approached, when it recommenced its movements, while she was also attracted by the frame. Thinking she was bewitched or possessed, her parents took her to the presbytery, that the spirit might be exorcised, or cast out. The curate, being a sensible man, objected, but set himself to work to observe the phenomenon, and being satisfied of the facts of the case, he bade them take her to a physician.

"Meanwhile, the intensity of the influence, whatever it was, augmented; not only articles made of oak, but all sorts of things, were acted upon by it, and reacted upon her, while persons who were near her, even without contact, frequently felt *electric* shocks. The effects, which were diminished when she was on a carpet or a waxed cloth, were most remarkable when she *was on the bare earth*. They sometimes entirely ceased for three days, and then recommenced. Metals were not affected. Any thing touching her apron or dress would fly off, although a person held it; and Monsieur Herbert, while seated on a heavy tub or trough, was raised up with it. In short, the only place she could repose on was a stone covered with cork. They also kept her still by isolating her. When she was fatigued the effects diminished. A needle, suspended horizontally, oscillated rapidly with the motion of her arm, without contact; or remained fixed while deviating from the magnetic direction. Great numbers of enlightened medical and scientific men witnessed these phenomena, and investigated them with every precaution to prevent imposition. She was often hurt by the violent involuntary movements she was thrown into, and was evidently afflicted by chorea, or St. Vitus's dance."—*Night Side of Nature*, page 382.

"The French paper mentions the circumstance that while Angelique was at work in the factory, "the cylinder she was turning was suddenly thrown a considerable distance without any visible cause; that this was repeated several times; that all the young girls in the factory fled, and ran to the curate to have him exorcise the young girl, believing she had a devil." After the priest had consigned her to the physician's care, the physician, with the father and mother, brought Angelique to Paris. M. Arago received her, and took her to the observatory, and in the presence of MM. Laugier and

Goujon made the following observations, which were reported to the Paris Academy of Sciences:—

"*First.* It is the left side of the body which appears to acquire this sometimes attractive, but more frequently repulsive, property. A sheet of paper, a pen, or any other light body, being placed upon a table, if the young girl approaches her left hand, even before she touches it, the object is driven to a distance as by a gust of wind. The table itself is overthrown the moment it is touched by her hand, or even by a thread which she may hold in it.

"*Second.* This causes instantaneously a strong commotion in her side, which draws her towards the table; but it is in the region of the pelvis that this singular repulsive force appears to concentrate itself.

"*Third.* As had been observed the first day, if she attempted to sit, the seat was thrown far from her, with such force that any other person occupying it was carried away with it.

"*Fourth.* One day a chest upon which three men were seated was moved in the same manner. Another day, although the chair was held by two very strong men, it was broken between their hands.

"*Fifth.* These phenomena are not produced in a continued manner. They manifest themselves in a greater or less degree, and from time to time during the day; but they show themselves in their intensity in the evening, from seven to nine o'clock.

"*Sixth.* Then the girl is obliged to continue standing, and is in great agitation.

"*Seventh.* She can touch no object without breaking it or throwing it upon the ground.

"*Eighth.* All the articles of furniture which her garments touch are displaced and overthrown.

"*Ninth.* At that moment many persons have felt, by coming in contact with her, a true electrical shock.

"*Tenth.* During the entire duration of the paroxysms, the left side of the body is warmer than the right side.

"*Eleventh.* It is affected by jerks, unusual movements, and a kind of trembling which seems to communicate itself to the hand which touches it.

"*Twelfth.* This young person presents, moreover, a peculiar sensibility to the action of the magnet. When she approaches the north pole of the magnet she feels a violent shock, while the south pole produces no effect; so that if the experimenter changes the poles, but without her knowledge, she always discovers it by the difference of sensations which she experiences.

"*Thirteenth.* The general health of Angelique is very good. The extraordinary movements, however, and the paroxysms observed every evening, resemble what one observes in some nervous maladies."

"The great fact demonstrated in this case," says E. C. Rogers, "is, that, under *peculiar conditions*, the human organism gives forth a physical power which, *without visible instruments*, lifts heavy bodies, attracts or repels them according to a law of polarity, overturns them, and produces the phenomena of sound. So far as the mere movement of objects, even of great weight, in connection with certain persons, is concerned, whether in the phenomena of the so called 'spiritual manifestations,' or out of them, the immediate agent is a physical one, and is identical throughout. None but the most ignorant can deny this." For a further delineation of the facts in this case, and deductions therefrom, we refer the reader to the work of Mr. Rogers, on the Dynamic Laws and Relations of Man.

"The next case we shall refer to is that of Frederica Hauffe, of the town of Prevorst, in the mountainous parts of Germany. It was found that in her hands, at a very early age, the hazel wand pointed out metals and water. It was also found that, in certain localities, the influences from the earth had a very powerful effect upon her susceptible nerves. It was frequently observed by the one she often accompanied in his walks through solitary places, that though she was skipping ever so gayly by his side, at certain spots a kind of seriousness and shuddering came over her, which for a long time he could not comprehend. He also observed that she experienced the same sensations in churchyards, and in churches where there were graves; and that, in such churches, she never could remain below, but was obliged to repair to the galleries. Superstition, it is true, has always claimed such facts as parts of her ghostly superstructure; but they are too material for this.

Frederica was almost constantly in a magnetic state, and in this condition frequently communicated what was taking place at a distance, and was aware of producing sounds in space, and some ways off; but this being found to materially injure her, the habit was abandoned. She had a very high degree of susceptibility to mundane influences, and the effect was, that mineral loads and subterranean currents acted through her upon a simple stick held in her hand.

At one time she was attacked with nervous fever, which continued fourteen days with great violence. This was followed by *seven years of* MAGNETIC LIFE, interrupted only by very short and merely apparent intervals. After the fever, she was attacked with spasms in the breast, which continued three days. On the second day, a peasant's wife came from the village, and seating herself beside her, said, "She needs no physicians; they cannot help her;" and laid her hands on her forehead. Immediately she was seized with the most direful spasms, and her forehead was as cold as if she was dead. During the whole night she cried deliriously that the woman had exercised a demoniacal influence upon her; and whenever the woman returned she was always attacked with spasms. On the third day they sent for a physician; and being then in a magnetic condition, she cried to him when he entered, although she had never seen him, "If you are a physician, you must help me!" He, well understanding her malady, laid his hands on her head; and it was remarked that, as long as he remained in the room, she saw and heard him alone, and was insensible to the presence of all other persons. The same kind of exclusive attachment has been seen in cases of persons who have fallen under the peculiar influence of the magnet or a crystal, thus showing the relation of mundane agencies to the psychological nerve centres, as well as to the nerve centres in the spine, and among the viscera.

After her physician had laid his hands on her she became calm, and slept for some hours. Some internal remedies and a bath were prescribed for her; but the spasms returned in the night, and for eighteen weeks she was attacked by them from twice to five or six times a day. All the remedies prescribed proving inefficacious, recourse was had to "magnetic passes," which, for a time, relieved the spasms. It was amid such sufferings and such influences that, in the month of February, 1823, after extreme tortures, she gave birth to her first child. This event was followed, for some time, by additional ills. The following is a somewhat curious circumstance, and goes to show the influence which one organization will have upon another, when a certain relation is established between them. It is this: The woman who, on a former occasion, had exerted so unhappy an influence upon the mother, produced precisely the same effects upon the child. Her contact with it threw it into spasms, and the convulsions became periodical until its death.

About a year after the birth of her child, being laughed at for her superstition, she was thrown into a state of rigid spasm, and became as cold and stiff as a corpse. For a long time no respiration was visible. She lay as in a dream. In this peculiar condition she spoke for three days entirely in verse and at another, she saw, for the same period, nothing but a ball of fire, that ran through her whole body as if on thin bright threads. And then, for three days, she felt as if water was falling upon her head, drop by drop; and it was at this time that she saw her own image. She saw it clad in white, seated on a stool, whilst she was lying in bed. She contemplated the vision for some time, and would have cried out, but could not; at length she made herself heard, and her husband entering, it disappeared. Her susceptibility was now so great that she *heard and felt what happened at a distance*, and was so sensible to external agencies, *that the nails in the walls affected her*, which obliged her friends to remove them. The least light had a powerful influence upon her nervous system, and could not be endured.

She was now induced to take a medicine which made her more calm, but threw her into a deeper trance. Still she could not endure the sunlight. She was taken in a darkened carriage to her home on the mountains. "Here she existed," says her physician, "only through the nervous emanation of others, and it became necessary that some one should always hold her hand; and if the person was weak, it increased her debility. The physician prescribed magnetic passes and medicines, but she fell into a magnetic sleep, *and then prescribed for herself.* Her greatest suffering arose from the sensation of having a stone in her head. It seemed as if her brain was compressed, and at every breath she drew, the motion pained her. At this time a large magnet was applied to her forehead; immediately her head and face were turned round, and her mouth distorted as by a stroke of palsy. On the 28th of December she gave birth to her second child, which was followed, as before, by a long and severe illness. She continued constantly in a magnetic state. Persons of various tempers now became her magnetizers. The effects of these different nervous temperaments upon hers were very serious. It brought her into special relation to so many persons, that, even *at a distance, they affected her, visions of whom would appear to her like visions of spirits.* This, moveover, brought her into a deeper magnetic condition, and rendered her more *dependent on the nervous energy of others.* Another physician was employed from a distance. He gave her an amulet to wear, composed of certain substances, and a small magnet, all arranged together. Occasionally this amulet, untouched by any one, would run about her head, breast, and bed covering, like a live thing."

"It has already been remarked, that, in the earlier stage of her magnetic state, she was aware of *making sounds at a distance.* This she repeatedly performed, so that her friends at a distance, as they lay in bed, *heard distinctly the sounds.* This fact being communicated to her physician, Dr. Kerner, he, by actual experiment and observation, confirmed it. This was not performed by her will, which was inactive in her somnambulic or cataleptic state, as well as her consciousness. Every nerve centre was in a most intimate *rapport* or relation with the mundane agencies, especially that which acts in conjunction with the nervous force, and holds every animal in a certain connection with every thing out of the organism.

The father of this unfortunate woman inhabited a house which formed a part of an old cathedral, where, it had been reported by former tenants, *strange sights had been seen, and strange sounds heard.* It was in this house, at the time of her somnambulic state, already spoken of, that there were heard *unusual knockings on the walls, noises in the air*, and other sounds, which, as Dr. Kerner remarks, "can be testified to by more than twenty credible witnesses." *There was a trampling up and down stairs by day and by night to be heard, but no one to be seen, as well as knockings on the walls and in the cellars; but, however suddenly a person flew to the place to try to detect whence the noise proceeded, they could see nothing. If they went outside, the knocking was immediately heard inside, and vice versa.* The noises at length became so perplexing, that her father declared that he could live in the house no longer. They were not only audible to every body in the house, but to the passengers in the street, who stopped to listen to them as they passed. Whenever there was playing on the piano, and singing, sounds would commence on the walls."

We have not room to mention all the facts in her case; but will add a few of the most remarkable. "She was very susceptible to *electrical influences*, and, what is almost incredible, *she had a preternatural feeling* or *consciousness of human writing*. Various minerals seemed to have a specific effect, when brought in contact with her. *Glass and rock crystal* had a powerful effect in waking her from the somnambulic state, or in exciting the force within her organism. This fact, and others of this character in abundance, point to the peculiar tendency of this force, in some cases of disease, to act outwardly from the nerve centres upon glass ware, window glass, &c. "We have known a child, eight years old," says Mr. Rogers, "who seldom, at one period, took hold of a glass dish without its soon bursting to pieces." In the case of Frederica, a rock crystal, placed on the pit of her stomach, and allowed to remain there for some time, would produce a deep state of catalepsy. She was affected in the same manner by silicious sand and gravel, or even by standing some time near a glass window. If she chanced to seat herself on a sandstone beach, she was apt to become cataleptic; and once, having been for some time missed, she was at length found at the top of the house, seated on a heap of sand, so rigid, that she was unable to move away from it. Whenever she was placed in a bath by her medical attendants, it was with a great deal of labor they could immerse her body beneath the surface. Her specific gravity seemed to be more like cork, or a bladder of air, than that of muscle, nerve, and bone. Something seemed to pervade her body, or to act upon it, so entirely opposite to the centripetal action of the earth, as to counteract this law of force in the most marked manner. This fact suggested to Dr. Kerner a curious experiment, which resulted in the development of another important phenomenon. He had concluded, that as all these phenomena had taken place more or less in conjunction with those usually termed *magnetic* or *mesmeric*, there might be some relation of the forces in both, or indeed they might be identical. To test this matter, he at one time placed his fingers against hers, when he found at once there existed a mutual attraction, as between two magnets; and now, by extending his hand upward, *he raised her clear from the ground; thus she was suspended, as a magnet suspends a piece of iron,* or *another magnet, simply by a polar force.* This was repeated several times, and afterwards his wife did quite the same thing."

"We have already spoken of the action which the sun's light had upon her in producing physical effects. Among others it was observed that the different colored rays produced each a specific effect. The light of the moon, also, when she looked at it, produced coldness and shivering, with melancholy." The effects of these agents on the human organism are clearly explained, in the numbers of an astronomical paper, by Mr. Chapman, of Philadelphia.

"On touching Frederica with a finger, during an electrical state of the atmosphere, she saw small flashes, which ascended to the ceiling; from men these were colorless, from women blue; and she perceived emanations of the same kind, and of the same variation of color, from people's eyes."

Concerning the power possessed in the nerve centres of this woman, to produce sounds at a distance, Dr. Kerner remarks as follows: "As I had been told by her parents, before her father's death, that, at the period of her early magnetic state, she was able to make herself heard by her friends, as they lay in bed at night, in the same village, in other houses, by a knocking,—as is said of the dead,—I asked her, in her sleep, whether she was able to do so now, and at what distance. She answered that she could sometimes do it. Soon after this, as we were going to bed, (my children and servants being already asleep,) we heard a knocking, as if in the air over our heads; There were six knocks, at intervals of half a minute. It was a hollow, yet clear sound, soft, but distinct. We were certain there was no one near us, nor over us, from whom it could proceed; and our house stands by itself. On the following evening, when she was asleep, (we had mentioned the knocking to nobody whatever,) she asked me whether she should soon knock to us again; which, as she said it was hurtful to her, I declined." And yet, not long after this, Kerner relates the following, as having taken place at his house: "On the morning of the 23d of March, 1837, at one o'clock, I suddenly awoke, and heard seven knocks, one after another, at short intervals, seeming to proceed from the middle of my chamber: my wife was awakened also; and we could not compare this knocking to any ordinary sound. Mrs. Hauffe lived several houses distant from us."

"On the 30th of the same month, Rev. Mr. Hermann came into *rapport* or special relation with Mrs. H., through the medium of psychological sympathy, as well as through the physical influence. Previous to this he had not been troubled with strange sounds at his house, but after that period he was awakened every night, at a particular hour, by a knocking in his room,—sometimes on the floor, and sometimes on the walls,—which his wife heard as well as himself. In a great part of her magnetic state, Mrs. H. was under a strong state of religious feeling, and was often engaged in prayer. Rev. Mr. Hermann sympathized with her in this, and with the commencement of the rapping in his room, he experienced an involuntary disposition to pray." (See Mr. Rogers's work, where many such cases are given.)

In elucidation of the effect of glass, sand, gravel, &c., upon her organism, we will state an additional fact, as related by her physician: "On the 21st of April, Dr. K. was at the house of Mrs. H. The window being open, he saw a quantity of gravel come in the window, which he not only saw, as he says, 'but picked it up!' To be certain that no one threw it in, he immediately looked out. On comparing it, he found it to be such gravel as lay in the front of the house."

"Now, let the phenomena we have related be put side by side with those which occurred at the house of Rufus Elmer, in Springfield, Massachusetts, on the 5th of April, 1852, as witnessed by Professor Wells, of Cambridge, and others, and alleged to be the work of spirits.

First. The table was moved in every possible direction, and with great force, when no cause of motion could be perceived.

Second. The table was forced against each one present so powerfully as to move them from their positions, together with the chairs they occupied, in all several feet.

Third. Mr. Wells and Mr. Edwards took hold of the table in such a manner as to exert their strength to the best advantage, but found the invisible power, exercised in the opposite direction, to be quite equal to their utmost efforts.

Fourth. In two instances, at least, while the hands of all the members of the circle were placed on the top of the table, and while no visible power was employed to raise the table, or otherwise to move it from its position, it was seen to rise clear of the floor, and to float in the atmosphere for several seconds, as if sustained by a denser medium than the air.

Fifth. Mr. Wells was rocked to and fro with great violence, and at length it poised itself on two legs, and remained in this position for some thirty seconds, when no other person was in contact with the table.

Sixth. Three persons, Messrs. Wells, Bliss, and Edwards, assumed positions on the table at the same time, and while thus seated, the table was moved in various directions.

Seventh. Occasionally we were made conscious of the occurrence of a powerful shock, which produced a vibratory motion of the floor of the apartment. It seemed like the motion occasioned by distant thunder, or the firing of ordnance far away, causing the tables, chairs, and other inanimate objects, and all of us, to tremble in such a manner that the effect was both seen and felt.

In conclusion, it was observed that D. D. Hume, the medium, frequently urged the company to hold his feet and hands. The room was well lighted, and a lamp was placed on and under the table, and every possible opportunity afforded for the closest inspection. They were therefore positive that there was no deception in the case. The conclusion was, *that it must be the work of spirits*—a singular conclusion, indeed, for men of such standing and acquirements. It might all have been accomplished, *biologically*; but admitting the whole to be literally and substantially true, they fall far short of well-attested phenomena, where it was not so much as *conjectured* even to be *at all supernatural*."

The fact is incontrovertibly evident, that physical agents, subtile and unseen, are every where at work. "Force shows itself," as the elegant Somerville remarks, in his Connection of the Physical Sciences, "in every thing that exists in the heavens or on the earth." There is a physical power which not only binds satellites to their planet, and planets with suns, and sun with sun throughout the wide extent of creation, which is the cause of the disturbances, as well as the order of nature, but it physically binds man to man, and man to nature. And as every tremor it excites in one planet is immediately transmitted to the farthest limits of the system, in oscillations, which correspond in their periods with the cause producing them, like sympathetic notes in music, or vibrations from the deep tones of an organ, so every vibration, thus excited, is transmissible to the delicate centres of every organic being, provided the repulsive agent of those beings is changed in its relative condition so as to admit its influx. (See Geometry and Faith, by Rev. T. Hill, of Waltham.)

"It is well known to every chemist, that wherever there is chemical action going on, there is a constant evolution of some force. Now, that there is a constant chemical action taking place is certain, and the sources of this action are very numerous. Among others, we have that of water, (often holding in solution saline ingredients, thus increasing its action upon metallic substances,) which, percolating through the surface, acts upon all those surfaces whose materials have a strong chemical affinity for the oxygen or hydrogen of the water.

Wherever there is a mineral load the development of force is in some instances very great. For instance, Mr. R. W. Fox was able, by connecting two lodes with copper wires, and conducting the latter to the surface of the earth, and immersing them in a cell which contained a solution of sulphate of copper, to obtain an electrotype copy of an engraved copperplate.

Thus "the earth itself may be made a *battery*," as Robert Hunt says. "We know," he repeats, "that, through the superficial strata of the earth, electric currents circulate freely, whether they are composed of clay, sand, or any mixture of these with decomposed organic matter; indeed, that with any substance in a moist state, electric currents suffer no interruption." The electricity of mineral veins has attracted the attention of some of the first philosophers of Europe, and has led to some highly-interesting experiments with regard to the action of this important agent in the formation, disposition, and direction of rocks and mineral veins. M. Becqueral and others have made use of these currents successfully in imitating Nature in her processes of making crystals and other mineral formations."

"It is not, however, necessary to suppose that the agent of which we are treating particularly requires a chemical action to develop it, or the action of the electric force. Experiments have proved that it is developed in every form of material action—that even the substances of the earth, without sensible alteration, exert this force. To this agent the sensitive nerve centres are extremely susceptible. The celebrated Ritter, of Germany, devoted much time to an investigation of this subject, and, in 1809, published Supplementary Treatises upon it, together with Amoretti's celebrated work on the same subject—Physical and Historical Inquiries into Rhabdomancy, &c., in Germany. (See Dr. Ashburner's Translation of Rheinbach, first American edition; Redfield.) Schubert, in his work on Natural History, says, "It seems clear, from many observations, that the whole mineral (and much of the vegetable) kingdom *has a profound and mysterious relation with the organism of man.*" "*This* relation," says Rogers, "is that of matter with matter connected by an imponderable agent." "The phenomena which betray this, as a fact of nature, have been observable from the earliest ages. It is certain, however, that local causes often give developments to such strange phenomena, *that it requires all the science that can be mustered to keep back the tide of superstition which will be thus aroused in the breasts of those unacquainted with the action of these agents.*"

Some will ask the question, "If these things be true, why have we not heard of them before?" We confess that we know of no other possible reason than that such inquiries are not "*posted up*," as they should be, in matters of history and science. But, before closing this part of our subject, we propose to relate a few more incidents, by way of illustration.

"In the year 1849-50, certain highly-respectable houses in the city of New York seem to have been all at once unaccountably beset with a strange power, which seized upon particular parts, and would not allow any one, not even the members of the families, to touch those seemingly consecrated things. Whenever this was attempted, a loud, sharp sound would be instantly given, accompanied with a sharp and spiteful flash of light, as if the agent was determined to protect that which it had seized upon. But this was not all; it would smartly shock the intruder with a blow, as if with an unseen fist, or the like. It even seized upon the members of these families at times, and would—so to speak—make them apparently strike one another, in an unseen manner, simultaneously. It was often the case that a stranger could not call at the door without being instantly struck on the wrist or elbow, on touching the knob of the door bell; and he would see, at the same instant, an angry flash of light, as if from some demon's eye. The ladies were not allowed to kiss each other without each receiving, on the approach of their lips, a fiery smack, as from a spirit's lips. The dear little ones of these families were prevented from giving their mothers the parting salutation on retiring for the night."

"There *seemed* to be a great deal of cunning shown by this agency. If the lady of the house did not think to pay all due deference to its rules, when she wished to give orders to the servants below through the metallic speaking tube, she was sure to receive an unseen blow in the mouth, almost sufficient to stagger her: at the same instant she would see the flash of what might have been taken for a 'fiery,' if not for an 'evil eye.'"

"Professor Loomis visited these dwellings, (see Annual of Scientific Discovery, 1851, page 129,) and observed these phenomena. He perceived the flash whenever the hand was brought near to the knob of the door, also to the gilded frame of a mirror, the gas pipes, or any metallic body, especially when this body communicated freely with the earth. "In one house," says this scientific gentleman, in his description before the American Scientific Association, at New Haven, "in one house, which I have had the opportunity to examine, a child, in taking hold of the knob of a door, received so severe a shock that it ran off in great fright. In passing from one parlor to the other, if the lady of the house chanced to step upon the brass plate which served as a slide for the folding doors, she received an unpleasant shock in the foot. When she touched her finger to the chandelier, there appeared a brilliant spark, and a snap." After a careful examination of several cases of this kind, Professor Loomis came to the conclusion "that the electricity is created (excited) by the friction of the shoes of the inmates upon the carpets of the house." "If the professor is correct in his conjecture, it would follow that every house," says Mr. Rogers, "with similar carpets, should become electrized, and exhibit similar phenomena, in which case we should have observed their appearance at a much earlier period, and the occurrence would have been presented much more frequently and extensively. Yet the phenomena is every whit electrical; hence we are led by them to see, that when local circumstances are favorable, an agent may be developed in our midst, which may play the most singular pranks, which, it is more than probable, may be attributed to *supernatural*, and even to SPIRITUAL *powers*, if the witnesses should be ignorant of those characteristics which identify them with a well-known agent. Had the characteristics in the above been contrary to those of any known agent, although the phenomena had been entirely physical, how many would have leaped to the conclusion, without a moment's thought or investigation, that the force was a power of the invisible spirit world? With regard to the phenomena of the present day, reason has been entirely set aside; hence the precipitate conclusion concerning them, even by many who lay great claim to its use and application to all other subjects. We have been truly astonished at the course of such persons."

"We shall now present a few cases that bear a closer analogy to electricity, perhaps, than those we have been considering. The first we shall speak of is that of the two Smyrna girls, who visited France in 1839, and exhibited what was called *their electrical powers, in moving tables without contact*. The account was published in the Boston Weekly Magazine, of December 28, 1839. The two girls landed at Marseilles, about the first of November, 1839. In hopes of realizing a splendid fortune, they intended to exhibit themselves in France, and other parts of the continent. Immediately on their arrival, several persons, including several men of science and professors, visited them, and ascertained the following phenomena:—

First. "The girls stationed themselves, facing each other, at the ends of a large *table*, keeping at a distance from it of one or two feet, according to their electrical dispositions.

Second. "When a few minutes had elapsed, a *crackling*, like that of electric fluid spreading over gilt paper, was heard, when,—

Third. "The table received a strong shake, which always made it *advance from* the ELDER to the younger sister.

Fourth. "A *key*, *nails*, or any piece of *iron* placed on the table *instantaneously stopped* the phenomena.

Fifth. "When the iron was adapted to the *under part* of the table, it produced no effect upon the experiment.

Sixth. "Saving this singularity, the facts observed constantly followed the known laws of electricity, whether glass insulators were used, or whether one of the girls wore silk garments. In the latter case, the electric properties of both were neutralized." Such was the state of matters for some days after the arrival of the young Greeks; but,—

Seventh. "The temperature having become cooled, and the atmosphere having loaded itself with *humidity*, all perceptible electric virtue seemed to have deserted them. One may conceive the melancholy of these girls," the writer continues, "and the disappointment of the two Greeks, their relations, who came with them to share their anticipated wealth."

"In this case we have the "manifestation" of a force greatly analogous to that often witnessed at the present day. In one important respect it acted differently from electricity, in that it was broken by simply laying a *key* or a small piece of *iron* on the object the agent had acted upon, &c. "It must be admitted, however," says Mr. Rogers, "that the fact of the influence of glass insulators and the silk dress, causing a cessation of the phenomena, shows that the agent that acted upon the table was, in some way, a form of electricity, though greatly varying, in its laws of action, from that usually known to science. We have," says Mr. R., "some curious facts relating to this *modified agent*, to present from Matucci and others," (in the second number of our work.)

"From the effects of the humidity of the atmosphere, some may conclude that the agent must have been *electricity*, inasmuch as the same state of the atmosphere produces a like effect upon the action of friction electricity. Let us allow this, and turn to precisely the same phenomenon, as it has been manifested in the cases of numerous 'mediums' for the so-called '*spiritual manifestations.*'"

"We will not state it upon our authority alone, but also upon that of a large number of intelligent believers in the spiritual origin of these phenomena, that the electrical condition of the atmosphere enters into the circumstances of their evolution; that in a humid state of the weather it is not only difficult, in many instances, but sometimes it is absolutely impossible, to obtain them under such a condition." We know that many of the less informed "mediums" attribute these failures to the *capriciousness of the spirits*, and frequently scold them soundly for their misdemeanors, though at other times they seem to pity them because they get so weary and fatigued in answering so many inquiries, and being so long "*on duty.*"

"It was thought by some who witnessed the case of Angelique Cottin, that the agent which acted so powerfully from her organism, overthrowing tables, twisting chairs out of stout men's hands, raising a man in a heavy tub, was electricity. C. Crowe says it did cause the deviation of the magnetic needle; but M. Arago, who knows more about this abused agent than a nation of theorizers, could not detect the least signs of it by the nicest tests. And yet it would give the person who touched her or her dress a powerful shock, as if it *were* electricity. Still, it may be the same agent that is ground out of plate glass, that propagates news from city to city on iron wires, and that thunders in the material heavens."

"It has been supposed that because, in many instances, 'mediums' have given shocks like those given by electrized bodies, the two agents must be identical. Not long since, a young lady, about sixteen years of age, Miss Harriett Bebee, was placed in a magnetic state, in company with Mrs. Tamlin, both being of a clairvoyant character. The sounds were heard while they were in that state. Every time these occurred a very sensible jar, like an electric shock, was experienced by Miss Bebee. In answer to a question, she stated that at each sound she felt as if there was electricity passing over her. Several of the persons, in whose presence these sounds are heard, always receive a slight shock, so that there is a slight jar, which has sometimes been so plain as to lead persons, ignorant of the facts and the phenomenon, to accuse them of making it themselves." Says a writer upon this subject, "This feeling of electricity seems to pervade nearly every thing connected with these phenomena. When the rapping is heard, the peculiar jar is felt, differing from the jar produced by a blow; and in various other ways we are reminded of the use of this subtile agent. We often see, in a dark room, bright electric flashes on the wall and other places."

The same writer observes, "Persons sometimes feel a sensation of electricity passing over their limbs when they stand in the vicinity of those who get the sounds most freely, although the particular persons who seem to be the mediums feel no sensation at all. In one or two instances we have seen a perceptible shock, as if caused by a galvanic battery, especially when the persons were under the influence of magnetism."

"In a work published in Cincinnati, by "William T. Coggshall, the author says, "We have felt positive electrical influences from clairvoyants. At the present time," he continues, "what is termed 'electrical circles' are being formed every week in Cincinnati, for the benefit of persons whose systems require additional electrical power. We have seen several women so powerfully electrized in these circles, that the same effects were produced upon them which would have been had they been isolated in connection with a galvanic battery." So it has been seen that, on touching Angelique Cottin, a person would receive a "true electric shock." This kind of shock was experienced by Campeti and Bleton, in passing over mineral veins and subterraneous streams, as mentioned by Dr. Ashburner. "Many somnambulic persons," says C. Crowe, "are capable of giving an electric shock; and I have met with one person, not somnambulic, who informed me that he has frequently been able to do it by an effort of the will."

"When an iron plate was brought near to one of Reichenbach's patients, and a crystal brought in contact with it, the effect upon it was like an electric shock, which even ascended from the elbow to the shoulder." Many other cases might be cited to the same purpose. The magnet and iron have a specific action upon the nervous system; and the same agent acts also from crystals, vegetable substances, and the human hand, nay, from the earth itself." The second number of Mr. Rogers's work contains some interesting facts of this character.

"Vitality," says Dr. W. E. Channing, in his Notes on Electricity, "is dependent on physical conditions, and performs its functions by the agency of physical forces." The Rev. Thomas Hill, in his Fragmentary Supplement to the Ninth Bridgewater Treatise, observes that "all bodies are moved through the agency of other bodies, and we see nowhere a motion which is not dependent upon *physical causes*, that is, which is not produced by *physical agents*. Our will employs, unconsciously, the aid of nerve and muscle; the supreme will employs, with wise designs, the intervention of the laws of *impulse, attraction*, and *repulsion*." "When, in the course of ages, the comparative easy problems of astronomy were solved, problems of more difficulty were brought to view. Phenomena which were not *obvious*, not *pictured alphabet*, but the *fine print of creation, electrical, optical*, and *chemical phenomena*, led men into more *hidden* knowledge."

"The agents employed by the animal organization," says Dr. Channing, "are principles found UNIVERSALLY IN NATURE, and, in addition to these, a force which is peculiar to living structures—the special agent of vitality." "Now, it might reasonably be expected, that if electricity, among other agents found "universally in nature," is also associated with the agent of the animal economy, it might, under favorable conditions, exhibit its characteristic phenomena. These conditions would, of course, be owing to a variation of the organism from its normal standard. The following case, given by Dr. Ennemoser, of Germany, exhibits some of these characteristics:—

The case was that of a young woman, sister of a professor at Strasburg. Immediately on a sudden fright, she was seized with a nervous malady, which continued for a long period, and finally terminated in her death. Among the remarkable symptoms in her case were the following:—

First. Those of *somnambulism*, with more or less lucidity.

Second. Her body became so highly charged with electricity that it was necessary to conduct it away by a regular process of conduction.

Third. Her body would impart powerful shocks to those who came in contact, and even when they did not touch her.

Fourth. She controlled its action so as to give her brother (the professor) a "smart shock when he was several rooms off." (The account states, that when the professor received the shock, "he started up and rushed into her chamber, where she was in bed; and as soon as she saw him, she said, laughing, 'Ah, you felt it, did you?'")

Fifth. She was subject, also, to spasms and paroxysms of rigor and trembling.

Some of the phenomena, in this case, resemble those we see exhibited by the electric fish. The case is an important one in considering the command which the nerve centres possess over the general agents associated with them."

We shall now present another singular case, which occurred in this country, in the month of January, 1839, an account of which was given in Silliman's Journal, by a correspondent:—

First. That "on the evening of January 28, 1839, during a somewhat extraordinary display of the northern lights, a respectable lady became so highly charged with electricity, as to give out vivid electrical sparks from the end of each finger, to the face of each of the company present."

Second. That this did not cease with the heavenly phenomena, but continued several months, during which time she was constantly charged and giving off electrical sparks to every conductor she approached. This was extremely vexatious, as she could not touch the stove, or any metallic utensil, without giving off an electrical spark, with the consequent twinge.

Third. That "the state most favorable to *this phenomena* was an atmosphere of about eighty degrees Fahrenheit, moderate exercise, and social enjoyment. It disappeared in an atmosphere approaching zero, and under the debilitating effects of fear."

Fourth. That, "when seated by the stove, reading, with her feet upon the fender, she gave sparks at the rate of three or four a minute; and under the most favorable circumstances, a spark that could be seen, heard, or felt, passed every moment."

Fifth. That "she could charge others in the same way, when insulated, who could then give sparks to others."

Sixth. "To make it satisfactory that her dress did not produce it, it was changed to cotton, and woollen, without altering the phenomenon. The lady is about thirty, of sedentary pursuits, and delicate state of health, having, for two years previously, suffered from acute rheumatism and neuralgic affections."

For further investigation into the cause of singular phenomena evolved from secret agents, and the true philosophy of biology, magnetism, trance, &c., we would again refer to the numbers of a work by Mr. Rogers, now in process of publication. His principles and deductions challenge successful contradiction.

EXPERIMENTS IN BIOLOGY.

Biology, so called, is one peculiar feature, or form, of mesmerism. "These experiments," says Dr. Richmond, "attracted much attention some three years since, in Ohio, and other places, and such was the intense excitement of the public mind that, in some places, parents and the public were obliged to interfere and stop children from biologizing each other." It was found that not only muscular motion, but the exercise of the senses, could be destroyed by the will of the operator. Taste was obliterated, or changed, memory destroyed, and any picture presented to the mind of the subject would be seen. Tell him he saw snakes, and he would become frightened, and rush with violence over the seats and benches. Tell him he was sleigh riding, and he would instantly seize the reins, and drive the horses with great glee. Tell him he was a witch—an old woman in rags—and he would own the character, and confess all the crimes with which you had charged him. Tell him he was a gay young lady, and another subject was about to court him, and a love scene would commence. Tell him he was cold, and he would shiver, his teeth chatter; he would stamp, and thresh his hands to keep them warm. Tell him it was summer—very hot, and he would begin fanning himself, fling off his coat, and, unless prevented, would divest himself of all garments tell him that a tree of fruit was before him, and he would begin to fill his pockets. Sweep the room before him, and open the sky, and say that the river of life and a white throne were before him, that the judgment was set, and instantly he would assume the attitude of devotion; he would gaze with burning eye and rapt delight into the scene of glory. Take him to a lake side, tell him a child was drowning in the water, and he would wade in, take it in his arms, and lay it carefully down, and weep over it in deep pity. Bring before him the lightning's flash, the thunder's roll, or proclaim a God in grandeur, and a world on fire, and, as once actually took place in Covington, Kentucky, a dozen subjects fell in intense fright: some on to the floor, some on benches, others sought to fly, and all declared to the audience that a shower of fire seemed to be around them. Any image the operator sees fit to plant in the subject's mind is readily done; any passion readily assumed; reverence, revenge, vanity, love, hate, fear, mirth, joy, grief, or ecstasy, are all *imitated* at his bidding, and safely dispersed and reproduced with the rapidity of thought, changing in an instant both the actions and motions of the subject. Tell the person he is suffocating in water, and he *will* suffocate, unless you prevent him. Tell him he is struck on the head, and he falls, as if stricken down with a hammer. No doubt a subject might be killed by a mental impression—by saying to him he was shot through the heart, or was struggling in water. This is the opinion of all operators in the art. The subject at the time is, to all appearance, in a perfectly *normal state*; his mental, moral, and physical powers seem unchanged, and he thinks at the time he can resist your power over him; he but gives you his eye, and you lead him captive by mental impressions. The only perceptible variation from the normal state is, that the *eye*, in most subjects, is clear and glassy, the same eye that is observed in some maniacs, and in consumptive patients—clear, sharp, and fearful to look at. The hidden fires of the soul seem to burn through it, with intense force. I have watched it for months, and years, in consumptives, under the wasting of vitality; and the eye kindles and sparkles with more intensity as they near their end. All impressible subjects have this eye, to a greater or less extent; all consumptives have it, as well as those who in early life are inclined to consumption.

The facts and incidents under the effects of biology are truly singular and wonderful; and yet the advocates of the "spirit mania" admit there is nothing supernatural in them. For aught we can see, the phenomena put forth by the "rappers" differ not materially from the biologic developments. They seem to be identical with each other.

I know it is affirmed that the developments of electro-biology do not cover the whole ground in dispute, inasmuch as *men and women only* are found to yield to its impressions, while *chairs, tables*, and other inanimate objects remain unimpressed. But if chairs and tables are not moved by one form of magnetism, they are by another, as we have abundantly shown. And any one with half an eye cannot but see that it would require less effort to move a table, or other inanimate object, than living, intelligent beings, capable of exerting their will in opposition to the effort. Dr. Richmond says he has "seen an operator draw a dozen persons from their seats, by the magnetic force of his hand, at the distance of many feet. The first move of the hand would bring the head forward, then the body, and by adding his voice, 'You will stand up,' they would, *while resisting with the will, in spite of themselves*, stand up, and follow his hand around the room." If biologists have not usually exerted their power upon inanimate things, it has probably been because they did not deem it of sufficient importance. We have seen, however, a biologist raise a table to the ceiling of a room, kindly permitting it to stick there a while, to the no small amusement of the spectators! And it can be done again. By the way, we would inquire what biologist is it that has sometimes lent his aid in the raising of tables, at a "circle" in East Boston, himself an unbeliever in "*spirit table-liftings?*"

The editor of the Spiritual Telegraph says, that "in the biological experiments there is a *visible human operator*," but, "in the spiritual manifestations, no human operator can be found, or demonstrated to exist." But, pray, what is the "medium," in these manifestations, but *a visible human operator?* Sometimes it takes three or four persons to produce a single demonstration. And sometimes they cannot muster *force* enough to do this, especially if the weather be rainy. And this is probably the reason why the rappers at Poughkeepsie have resolved not to admit unbelievers, nor at any time more than two or three new-comers, at a "circle," making, with the believers, ten or twelve in all—successful results never being guaranteed to those invited to attend.

Mr. Brittan himself asserts that it is "the same power that moves the *human medium* that also moves the *wooden table*," &c. Here we have a *human medium* that is *moved to do something*, and *wooden tables*, also; and if we can discover the secret agent in the one case, we shall likewise in the other, for there is a perfect sameness or coincidence in their operations. It is the same *unseen* power, in both cases, moving chairs, tables, tubs, troughs, bedsteads, and piles of lumber, besides other gross, ponderable bodies—cutting up an infinite variety of pranks to the *consternation* of some, and the *amusement* of others, as A. J. Davis says of the dancing plates, knives and forks, shovel, tongs, and poker, moved by "electrical discharges and magnetic attractions," or emanations of vital electricity seeking its equilibrium in the atmosphere.

FACULTY OF IMITATION.

The faculty of imitating signatures, of writing music, poetry, specimens of foreign tongues, &c., is no more strange than imitating the voice and gestures of those we never heard nor saw. Persons of scarcely any education or talents, while under biological influence, have been made to imitate the voice of Webster, Everett, Fillmore, and others, delivering off-hand speeches of most impassioned diction and eloquence; while, in their *normal* state, they could scarcely frame a paragraph in the king's English, much more deliver a formal address, embellished with a profusion of metaphors, tropes, and figures, accompanied with the finished attitudes and movements of a Choate, a Sumner, or a Banks! These mesmeric imitations refer also to mechanical and artistic power, and every talent that characterizes us as intelligent beings. Some assert that mediums are in a *perfectly normal state* during the exhibitions of the "spirit" phenomena; and yet, to the practical mesmerizer, nothing is plainer than that they are most absolutely mesmeric persons.

The power of *imitation* among mediums is various, but distinct. Some draw *maps*, purporting to come from a deceased schoolmate. Others draw *likenesses*; others speak in voices imitating the dead—but they can imitate the living just as well; others hear sounds—the voice of a wife, or child, or friend. Walter Scott relates the case of an English gentleman who was ill, and was told by his physician that he had lived in London too long, and *lived too fast*; and advised him to retire to the country and ruralize. One of his troubles was, that a set of *green* dressed dancers would enter his drawing room, go through their evolutions, and retire. He knew it was an illusion, but could not resist the annoyance, or the impressions made on him. He returned to his country seat, and, in a few weeks, got rid of his visitors. He concluded to remain out of town, and sent to London for the furniture of his old parlor, to be placed in his country house; but when it came, and was arranged in the room, the *corps de ballet*, dressed in *green*, all rushed into the room, *exclaiming*, "Here we are all again!" He had associated in his mind the furniture and the dancing apparitions, and when it returned, they came with it, and, as he thought, *spoke with voices*. We recollect of reading in a medical paper, published in Boston, an account of a man who believed his house to be haunted by the devil, in consequence of which he resolved to vacate it and remove into the country. His goods were packed into a wagon, and he was just upon the point of starting with his load, when to his surprise he heard a voice, seemingly among the goods, crying out, "We are all going together." "If that is the case," said the man, "I will unload again; for if I am *to have* the devil's company, it may as well be in one place as another."

The excessive use of wine will induce a state of the brain, in which the person thinks he hears voices and sees spirits; but on close examination it will be found that it is the work of the abnormal powers, developed in the brain by stimulating agents or intense thinking. It will be recollected that Swedenborg, after eating a late, heavy supper, heard a voice crying out to him in terrible accents, "Eat not so much." (See chap. 5.) Such phenomena may unravel the voice Judge Edwards heard. His long-continued meditation on death, with night, solitude, loneliness, and grief, had so impressed him that he thought he heard a sound in exact imitation of the voice of his wife. In the case related by Scott, hearing was not only affected, but the organ of color was involved in the hallucination, and the *green figures* were as plain before him as real persons. This is always one of the phenomena of ghost-seeing that the seer associates with the spectre, namely, *form* and *color*, *voice* and *action*.

The cases of imitation referred to, and others of the same class, are the results of the *imitative mechanic power* of the individual, brought out by the abnormal magnetic state existing at the time. For instance, if the individual has time and tune—the faculty of music within lying undeveloped—it may be brought out, and made to act, by the effects of magnetism. Last winter we listened to a lecture delivered in Newark, New Jersey, by the Rev. Mr. Harris, from New York city. He stated that there was a lady in Providence, who, by the agency of spirits, produced musical compositions equal to the productions of the best masters, as Haydn, Beethoven, and others, and that a volume of these pieces were soon to be issued from the press. And although the said work has not been heard of as yet, still we doubt not that a person in a magnetic state might write very good music, even if totally ignorant of its rules, as this young lady was said to be.

Phrenologists often tell persons that they would make excellent tailors, dressmakers, poets, painters, musicians, &c.—persons who never attempted to operate in these callings. "All they need," it is said, "is an opportunity for the development of their powers." Now, magnetism tends to develop or rouse these *dormant* faculties into action. It also gives a far-reaching, a far-seeing grasp and perception of things, as in the case of Miss Martineau, who, be it remembered, was too intelligent to attribute such effects to the agency of spirits.

A marked case of the increase of the *imitative power* of persons in the magnetic condition, is found in the case of Frederica Hauffe. In one of her magnetic moods she informed Dr. Kerner that she would make a diagram of the spheres. "The sun sphere," as she called it, is very complex; but "she spun out the complicated web with unerring precision," and a pair of compasses given her to facilitate her labor only embarrassed her. It is made up of circles within circles, and sections and points, amounting to thousands, related and connected; and yet the "whole was executed," says Dr. K., "in an incredible short space of time." An engraving was made of this sphere, and a year after she was shown the engraving, and said it was not correct; a point on one of the lines was wanting. On referring to the original, they found she was right. This diagram contained many curious things, and in some parts related to the highest departments of mathematics. This *faculty* she only possessed in the magnetic state, being wholly incompetent to the task when not clairvoyant. No living artist can execute that diagram with a pen, with a fac-simile before him, with the rapidity with which that ignorant, unlettered child of nature did it. "I have, in many cases," says Dr. Richmond, "witnessed this imitative power of mediums with the pen, dashing off figures and images with a rashness and rapidity almost inconceivable." As far as we can see, there is no more proof of the agency of spirits in one case than in the other; and we are sure no such claim was ever set up in the case of Mrs. Hauffe, though living in a less enlightened region, perhaps, than these United States. We might multiply cases of this kind, but space will not permit.

UNSEEN LETTERS AND SIGNATURES.

The operator in biology or magnetism often lays hold of the inquiring spectator, and uses him or her to imitate unseen letters, signatures, and sentences, in foreign languages. And no doubt but what Professor Bush has been made unconsciously instrumental in executing a few specimens of languages, his eyes wide open, it may be, all the while. It can be no more strange than that the son of Dr. Phelps should have been made unconsciously instrumental in tying himself to the limb of a tree in his father's yard, *supposing* it to have been done by *spirits*. (See the version of the affair by A. J. Davis.)

A biological mesmerist assures us that he finds no difficulty in raising beds, chairs, and tables; and in the case of Mr. Kellogg it is shown that such things are easily done without any aid from *spirits*. In the case of Dr. Taylor, the writing medium, it is shown, by the testimony of the spirits themselves, if their word is to be relied on, that the phenomena in his case were not done by spirits, but were the results of vital electricity. Such things are getting to be so common that we may expect soon to see the time when little ragged boys even (like those in Egypt, who went through the streets offering to show the spirit of any deceased friend for a penny or a piece of cake) will offer to lift tables, or imitate handwritings, at a penny a sight. We know of several "mediums," now engaged in these things, who confess they do not understand by what power it is they raise tables, or write sentences, &c., yet they do not believe it to be done by the agency of disembodied spirits. In many schools, the children have been forbidden by their teachers to indulge in these foolish practices. This power may be electricity, in some of its forms, or some other agent that has some relation or affinity to it, as in the cases related by Mr. Rogers.

A DANCING LIGHT.

A few years since the inhabitants of Southboro', Massachusetts, were excited and alarmed at the appearance of a *light*, about the size of a star, which for several successive nights was seen moving over a spot of land in the westerly part of the town. Upon examining the premises by daylight, it was found that a quantity of bones that had been buried in the earth had been thrown upon the surface by the roots of a tree, the trunk of which had recently been prostrated by a gale of wind. By many, these bones were supposed to belong to some human being, who, it was conjectured, had been murdered, and buried beneath the spot. And the light seen hovering near was considered indicative of such an event. But if the reader will turn to the second chapter of this work, he will learn that these *dancing lights*, so called, arise from an inflammable gas, evolved from decayed animal and vegetable substances, which take fire on coming in contact with atmospheric air. This *ignis fatuus*, *Jack-with-a-lantern*, or *Will-with-a-wisp* appearance is generally seen in dark nights, over boggy and marshy ground, and generally in motion, at the height of five or six feet, skipping from place to place, and frequently changing in magnitude and form. On some occasions, it is observed to be suddenly extinguished, and then to reappear at a distance from its former position. Those persons who have endeavored to examine it closely have found that it moves away from them with a velocity proportioned to that of their advance—a circumstance which has had no small influence on the fears of the ignorant and superstitious. Dr. Denham once saw an *ignis fatuus* in a boggy place, between two rocky hills, in a dark and calm night. He approached by degrees within two or three yards of it, and thereby had an opportunity of viewing it to the best advantage. It kept skipping about a dead thistle, till a slight motion of the air—occasioned, as he supposed, by his near approach—caused it to jump to another place; and as he advanced it kept flying before him. He observed it to be a uniform body of light, and concluded it must consist of *ignited vapor*. These appearances are common on the plains of Boulogne, in Italy, where they sometimes flit before the traveller on the road, saving him the expense of a torch on dark nights. Sometimes they spread very wide, and then contract themselves; and sometimes they float like waves, and appear to drop sparks of fire. They shine more strongly in rainy than in dry weather.

An appearance of the same kind is sometimes met with at sea, during gales of wind, and, of course, has become connected with many superstitious notions of sailors, who call it a *corpusant*. There are sometimes two together, and these are named Castor and Pollux. The following is a description of one, given by the voyager Dampier: "After four o'clock the thunder and the rain abated, and then we saw a corpusant, at our maintopmast head. This sight rejoiced our men exceedingly, for the height of the storm is commonly over when the corpusant is seen aloft; but when they are seen lying on the deck, it is generally accounted a bad sign. A corpusant is a certain small, glittering light; when it appears, as this did, on the very top of a mainmast, or at a yardarm, it is like a star; but when it appears on the deck, it resembles a great glowworm. I have been told that when the Spanish or Portuguese see them they go to prayers, and bless themselves for the happy sight. I have heard some ignorant seamen discoursing how they have seen them creep, or, as they say, travel about, in the scuppers, telling many dismal stories that happened at such times; but I did never see any one stir out of the place where it was first fixed, except on deck, where every sea washeth it about. Neither did I ever see any but when we had rain as well as wind, and, therefore, do believe it is some jelly."

The origin and nature of the lights above described have not yet been satisfactorily explained. More accurate observations than have been made are required to furnish the basis of a correct theory respecting them.

SAILORS' OMENS.

Sailors, usually the boldest men alive, are yet not unfrequently the very abject slaves of superstitious fear. Nothing is more common than to hear them talk of noises, flashes, shadows, echoes, and other visible appearances, nightly seen and heard upon the waters. Andrews, in his Anecdotes, says, "Superstition and profaneness, those extremes of human conduct, are too often found united in the sailor; and the man who dreads the stormy effects of drowning a cat, of whistling a contra dance while he leans over the gunwale, will, too often, wantonly defy his Creator by the most daring execrations and licentious behavior." Dr. Pegge says that "sailors have a strange opinion of the devil's power and agency in stirring up winds, which notion seems to have been handed down from Zoroaster, who imagined that there was an evil spirit, called *Vato*, that could excite violent storms of wind." To lose a cat overboard, or to drown one, or to lose a bucket or a mop, is, at the present day, a very unlucky omen with common sailors.

LOVE CHARMS.

Theocritus and Virgil both introduce women into their pastorals, using charms and incantations to recover the affections of their sweethearts. Shakspeare represents Othello as accused of winning Desdemona "by conjuration and mighty magic."

"Thou hast practised on her with foul charms;

Abused her delicate youth with drugs or minerals

That waken motion.

She is abused, stolen from me, and corrupted,

By spells and medicines bought of mountebanks."

In Gay's Shepherd's Week, these are represented as country practices:—

"Straight to the 'pothecary's shop I went,

And in love powders all my money spent.

Behap what will, next Sunday after prayers,

When to the alehouse Lubberkin repairs,

These golden flies into his mug I'll throw,

And soon the swain with fervent love shall glow."

In Love Melancholy, by Dr. Ferrand, it is said, "We have sometimes among us our silly wenches, some that, out of a foolish curiosity they have, must needs be putting in practice some of those feats that they have received by tradition from their mother perhaps, or nurse; and so, not thinking forsooth to do any harm, as they hope to paganize it to their own damnation. For it is most certain that *botanomancy*, which is done by the noise, or crackling, that box or bay leaves make when they are crushed between one's hands, or cast into the fire, was of old in use among the pagans, who were wont to bruise poppy flowers betwixt their hands, by this means thinking to know their loves." Speaking of the ancient love charms, characters, amulets, or such like periapses, Dr. F. says, "They are such as no Christian physician ought to use, notwithstanding that the common people do to this day too superstitiously believe and put in practice many of these paganish devices."

Miss Blandy, who was executed many years ago for poisoning her father, persisted in affirming that she thought the powder given her by her villanous lover, Cranston, to administer to him, was a "love powder," which was to conciliate her father's affection to her lover. She met her death with this asseveration; and her dying request, to be buried close to her father, seems a corroborating proof, that though she was certainly the cause of his premature death, yet she was not, in the blackest sense of the word, his wilful murderer.

We quote the following lines from Herrick's Hesperides:—

A CHARM OR AN ALLAY FOR LOVE.

"If so be a toad be laid

In a sheepskin newly flayed,

And that tied to a man, 'twill sever

Him and his affections ever"

EFFECTS OF A BELIEF IN A GHOST.

Whenever a real ghost appears,—by which we mean some man or woman dressed up to frighten another,—if the supernatural character of the apparition has been for a moment believed, the effects on the spectator have always been injurious—sometimes producing convulsions, idiocy, madness, or even instantaneous death. The celebrated Allston, the painter, when in England, related the following incident to his friend Coleridge, the poet: "It was, I think," said he, "in the University of Cambridge, near Boston, that a certain youth took it into his wise head to convert a Tom Paine-ish companion of his by appearing as a ghost before him. He accordingly dressed himself up in the usual way, having previously extracted the ball from the pistol which always lay near the head of his friend's bed. Upon first awakening, and seeing the apparition, the youth that was to be frightened very coolly looked his companion, the ghost, in the face, and said, 'I know you; this is a good joke; but you see I am not frightened. Now you may vanish.' The ghost stood still. 'Come,' said the youth, 'that is enough. I shall get angry; away!' Still the ghost moved not. 'By heavens!' ejaculated the young man, 'if you do not, in three minutes, go away, I'll shoot you.' He waited the time, deliberately levelled his pistol, fired, and with a scream at the immovability of the figure, became convulsed, and soon afterwards died. The very instant he believed it to be a ghost, his human nature fell before it."

THE INVISIBLE LADY.

In the year 1804, an invisible lady and acoustic temple were exhibited in Boston, as an "Extraordinary Aerial Phenomenon." Its body was made of glass It gave answers to questions asked by visitors. In London, a few years ago, there was shown an apparatus consisting of a four-footed stand, and several trumpet-mouthed tubes, from any one of which spectators received ready answers to questions. The answers were said to come from the "invisible girl;" but the true explanation of the puzzle was, that a secret tube, in the legs of the apparatus, communicated the sounds to a girl in a neighboring apartment. Probably something similar was arranged in the glass body exhibited in Boston; and if we mistake not, during the sojourn of Joice Heth, of more recent notoriety, at the Albany Museum, a shrewd Albanian, after a minute and diligent examination, made the wonderful discovery that the old lady, or *nurse of Washington*, was composed of *India rubber*, and was made to breathe, speak, cry, sing, &c., by the aid of *ventriloquism*!

In a case of spirit rappings, Professor Grimes discovered that the party had contrived to have some levers concealed beneath the floor, and by means of certain little pegs coming through where the rappers sat, connecting with the levers, all nicely poised on a balance, they placed their feet upon them, and produced the raps at pleasure. And in the case of the Rochester rappers, when their ankles were firmly held by the committee of investigation, it is said a servant girl rapped with her knuckles under the floor. Mrs. Culver, who had been instructed by the Fox family, and had practised with them a while, afterwards renounced the craft, and exposed this among other deceptions to the world. "The girl," she says, "was instructed to rap whenever she heard their voices calling for spirits."

SORCERERS IN THE EAST.

The operations of the men sorcerers in India are quite scientific. They set about their work in a business-like manner, and in sight of the house of their intended victim the mystic caldron begins to boil and bubble. The victim, however, is not to be terrified out of his senses. What are his enemy's fires and incantations to him? He takes no notice, and continues to live on as though there was not a sorcerer in the world. But that *smoke*: it meets his eye the first object every morning. That ruddy glare: it is the last thing he sees at night. That measured but inarticulate sound: it is never out of his ear. His thoughts dwell on the mystical business. He is preoccupied, even in company. He wonders what they are putting into the pot, and if it has any connection with the spasm that has just shot through him. He becomes nervous; he feels sick; he cannot sleep from thinking; he cannot eat for that horrid broth that bubbles forever in his mind. He gets worse and worse, and dies! But this empire of the imagination is beaten in Java, where it is supposed that a housebreaker, by throwing a handful of earth upon the beds of the inmates, completely incapacitates them from moving to save their property. The man who is to be robbed, on feeling the earth fall upon him, lies as motionless as if bound hand and foot. He is under a spell, which he feels unable to break.

SINGULAR METAMORPHOSES.

In the East, men are believed to be frequently metamorphosed—sometimes voluntarily, sometimes involuntarily—into tigers. The voluntary transformation is effected merely by eating a certain root, whereupon the person is instantly changed into a tiger; and when tired of this character, he has only to eat another, when, as quick as thought, he subsides from a tiger into a man. But sometimes mistakes happen. An individual of an inquiring disposition once felt a strong curiosity to know the sensations attendant on transformation; but, being a prudent man, he set about the transformation with all necessary precaution. Having provided himself with

"the insane root

That takes the reason prisoner,"

he gave one also to his wife, desiring her to stand by and watch the event, and as soon as she saw him fairly turned into a tiger, to thrust it into his mouth. She promised, but her nerves were not equal to the performance. As soon as she saw her husband fixed in his new form, she took to flight, carrying in her hand, in the confusion of her mind, the root that would have restored him to her faithful arms. And so it befell that the poor tiger-man was obliged to take to the woods, and for many a day he dined on his old neighbors of the village, but was at last shot, and *recognized*!

In this superstition will be seen the prototype of the wolf mania of mediæval Europe. In Brittany, men betook themselves to the forests in the shape of wolves, out of a morbid passion for the amusement of howling and ravening; but if they left in some secure place the clothes they had thrown off to prepare for the metamorphosis, they had but to reassume them to regain their natural forms. But sometimes a catastrophe, like that above related, took place: the wife discovered the hidden clothes, and carrying them home, in the innocent carefulness of her heart, the poor husband lived and died a *wolf*!

PERNICIOUS ERRORS RELATING TO HEALTH.

In a former part of this volume, we have spoken of several impositions upon the credulity of the public, in matters appertaining to health. The astrologists have told us that "some plants are only to be plucked at the rising of the *dogstar*, when neither sun nor moon shine, while others are to be cut with a golden knife, when the moon is just six days old." To some particular plants "a string must be fastened, a hungry dog tied thereto, who, being allured by the smell of roasted flesh set before him, may pluck it up by the roots." At one time, the vegetable oil of swallows was considered a potent remedy. It was prepared "by compounding twenty different herbs with *twenty live swallows*, well beaten together in a mortar." Another medicine was prepared from *the raspings of a human skull*; another from the *moss, growing on the head of a thief*, who had been gibbeted and left to hang in the air. In addition to these, we have had "*the powder of a mummy; the liver of frogs; the blood of weasels; an ointment made of sucking whelps; the marrow of a stag; and the thigh bone of an ox.*" And we have numerous modern nostrums scarcely better than these, by which the gullible public are often sorely victimized.

There are many opinions among the people, which prove highly deleterious in being carried into practice. For instance, that we must "stuff a cold to cure it," when the reverse of the case is the only safe mode of procedure. In a cold, the lungs are already loaded and congested with accumulations of muco-purulent matter, which is increased by taking large quantities of food.

Erroneous views, in regard to cleanliness, often lead to great mischief. There is a notion with some that dirt is really healthy, especially for children. This idea probably originated from the fact, that those children who are allowed to play in the dirt are often more healthy than those who are confined in the nursery or parlor. But it should be remembered that it is not *dirt* which promotes their health, but active exercise in the open air. This more than compensates for the injury sustained by the dirt. There is, however, something deceitful, after all, in the ruddy appearance of these children, who, like some four-footed animals, are allowed to wallow in mire and dirt; for they actually suffer more, not only from chronic, but from acute diseases, than children whose parents are in better circumstances. The pores of the skin, as we have shown in the Family Physician, published by us a few years since, cannot be closed with filth for any length of time, and the subject remain uninjured. It is true, some years may pass away before the bad effects appear; but in after life, scrofula, rheumatism, jaundice, and even consumption, often arise after the cause which first gave rise to them is forgotten, if indeed it were ever suspected. It is our candid opinion, that a larger part of the deaths that occur among children by typhoid, scarlet fever, and other baleful diseases, is owing to some defect in management, as to diet, air, dress, or exercise, which we will briefly show in this connection.

There are some, in adult life, who abstain wholly from external ablutions, and never think of washing their bodies from one year to another. Now, such persons must be considered, to say the least, to be of an uncleanly habit; and such a habit is not only unfavorable to health, but to morality. Mr. Wesley reckons cleanliness to be second only to godliness. We venture to affirm that he who is most guilty of personal neglect will generally be found the most ignorant and vicious. I am well acquainted with a whole family who neglect their persons *from principle*. They are a sort of *new lights* in religious things, and hold that the true Christian should "slight the hovel, as beneath his care." But there is a want of intelligence, and even of common refinement, in the family, that certainly does not, and *cannot*, add much to their own happiness or comfort, aside from the fact that it greatly annoys their neighbors.

We do not pretend to say but that there are some great and good persons who are slovenly in their general appearance; but these are only exceptions to a general rule. On the contrary, common observation teaches us that it is a distinguishing mark of low-bred rowdyism, and of vicious and intemperate habits, to see young men dressed in the most loose and careless manner. A person of refinement and cultivation would feel ashamed to appear in such a manner before the public gaze.

Neglect of proper ventilation leads to incomparable mischief. There are many persons who live through the day in closely confined and excessively heated apartments, and also sleep in small contracted bed rooms, without the least opportunity for a current of fresh air. Who can wonder that they rise in the morning with wearied limbs, languid and listless, with a furred tongue, parched mouth, and headache? They are continually subjected to inhaling, over and over, the poison, the miasma, of their own bodies, which cannot but result, in the end, to the great detriment of health. We are perfectly astonished, oftentimes, to see to what an extent such a thing is carried. Take this, in connection with eating improper and badly-cooked food, fat meats, gravies, and pastries, the want of suitable protection against atmospheric changes, and active exercise in the open air, and who can marvel at the prevalence of deadly fevers, consumption, or cholera even? It is only a matter of surprise that there are not ten deaths where there is now one.

Look at the quality of the meats purchased for use. It is now a common practice with farmers (in order to save the milk) to sell their calves for market as soon as born; and people eagerly purchase this immatured meat because afforded at a low price. Then look at the enormous quantities of *pork* consumed. Go past the sausage factories, in the cities of Jersey, and you behold it heaped in piles, ready for the work of the hundreds of "choppers," driven by steam. Then look into the groceries, see the array of pound sausage meat, and cheese heads, so called. A grocer in Newark city informed us, last winter, that sausage meat and buckwheat cakes formed three quarters of the aliment of the citizens. And in Paterson, New Jersey, in the hottest of the season, calves were lying upon the pavements, ready to be slaughtered, and almost as momentarily devoured, as occasion demanded. Even the poor fowls, their legs swollen with inflammation from the cords with which they were bound, and half famished for water and food, and fevered by fright and exposure, were readily purchased by men and women, to satisfy the cravings of a perverted appetite. When we behold such practices, we cannot think it strange that mortality should be so rife as it is at times, especially when the atmosphere is in a condition to affect the body in a predisposed state, favorable to the development of diseases, such as that of small-pox, cholera, fever and ague, scarlet and typhoid, (i.e., decomposing fever,) which is the concentration of all others. The food we eat may convey the disease within, and unless the state of our system is healthy and harmonious, the resisting power will not be equal to the force and action of the external elements, and consequently we shall become a prey to the contagion, whatever type or form it assumes. We are somewhat inclined to think that A. J. Davis (who is a physician by profession) is correct, when he says, "The atmosphere has had the cholera, more or less, for thirty years, and will continue to have it until there occurs a geological change in many portions of the earth; and from the atmosphere the disease has been, and is, communicated epidemically to the predisposed potato plant, and also to the human system." A late English writer remarks, that "certain diseases prevail at the approach of the equinoxes."

9 789361 470882